**New Directions for
Community Colleges**

Arthur M. Cohen
EDITOR-IN-CHIEF

Richard L. Wagoner
ASSOCIATE EDITOR

Edward Francis Ryan
MANAGING EDITOR

Governance in the Community College

Robert C. Cloud
Susan T. Kater
EDITORS

Number 141 • Spring 2008
Jossey-Bass
San Francisco

GOVERNANCE IN THE COMMUNITY COLLEGE
Robert C. Cloud, Susan T. Kater (eds.)
New Directions for Community Colleges, no. 141

Arthur M. Cohen, Editor-in-Chief
Richard L. Wagoner, Associate Editor

NEW DIRECTIONS FOR COMMUNITY COLLEGES (ISSN 0194-3081, electronic ISSN 1536-0733) is part of The Jossey-Bass Higher and Adult Education Series and is published quarterly by Wiley Subscription Services, Inc., A Wiley Company, at Jossey-Bass, 989 Market Street, San Francisco, California 94103-1741. Periodicals Postage Paid at San Francisco, California, and at additional mailing offices. POSTMASTER: Send address changes to New Directions for Community Colleges, Jossey-Bass, 989 Market Street, San Francisco, California 94103-1741.

SUBSCRIPTIONS cost $85.00 for individuals and $209.00 for institutions, agencies, and libraries in the United States. Prices subject to change. See order form at the back of book.

EDITORIAL CORRESPONDENCE should be sent to the Editor-in-Chief, Arthur M. Cohen, at the Graduate School of Education and Information Studies, University of California, Box 951521, Los Angeles, California 90095-1521. All manuscripts receive anonymous reviews by external referees.

New Directions for Community Colleges is indexed in CIJE: Current Index to Journals in Education (ERIC), Contents Pages in Education (T&F), Current Abstracts (EBSCO), Ed/Net (Simpson Communications), Education Index/Abstracts (H. W. Wilson), Educational Research Abstracts Online (T&F), ERIC Database (Education Resources Information Center), and Resources in Education (ERIC).

Microfilm copies of issues and articles are available in 16mm and 35mm, as well as microfiche in 105mm, through University Microfilms Inc., 300 North Zeeb Road, Ann Arbor, Michigan 48106-1346.

Contents

EDITORS' NOTES

There has been a resurgence in interest—from both scholars and practitioners—in governance over the past decade owing to a number of forces, including changes in federal and state support for higher education funding, increased enrollments, growing competition for students, and massive retirements among community college leadership (Amey, 2004; Davis, 2000; Ehrenberg, 2004; Hines, 2000; Pusser, Slaughter, and Thomas, 2006; Tierney, 2004). Critics have noted that "current community college governance suffers from poor design and poor execution" (Davis, 2000, p. 1). We suggest that the massive turnover in leadership throughout community colleges creates new opportunities for understanding and perhaps altering governance structures within the community college—changes vital to achieving its evolving mission.

Most higher education governance structures evolved in an environment of rapid, sustained growth, when budgets grew as fast as enrollments. These governance systems were decentralized and siloed, with little communication between entities. In recent years changing environmental conditions—economic, political, demographic, and social—have increased challenges facing higher education while needed resources have declined (Alfred and Carter, 1999; Benjamin and Carroll, 1998). However, little has changed in governance structures. Thus, "higher education's institutions and systems across the country are being forced to restructure themselves" in terms of decision making to address the problems currently facing higher education (Benjamin and Carroll, 1998, p. 93).

Governance is a complex topic, with horizontal and vertical layers, fluid processes influenced by "multiple claimants to authority" (Hines, 2000, p. 105). Although college governance is normally considered to be the purview of trustees, administrators, and faculty, new stakeholders are entering the governance arena as environmental conditions warrant—stakeholders ranging from students to part-time faculty, legislators, state accountability agencies, alumni, and local groups. External influences on community college governance have increased dramatically in recent years.

For this volume of *New Directions for Community Colleges* we have engaged authors with expertise in various aspects of governance to provide an overview of current issues and future directions related to the governance of community colleges. Best practices in governance are examined as they relate to finance, collective bargaining, economic development, and P–16 (or P–20) initiatives. Trends in governance are identified and analyzed.

In Chapter One, Marilyn J. Amey, Eric Jessup-Anger, and Jody Jessup-Anger set the stage for understanding governance in the community college—

which factors affect it and why it matters—along with a brief discussion of how community college governance differs from university governance. The authors review different governance models in community colleges as well as the role of academic senates, unions, and boards of trustees in community college governance, while placing these different models into political and economic contexts.

In Chapter Two, George E. Potter and Daniel J. Phelan examine institutional governance transformations over the past forty years (much of which George has witnessed over the forty-four years he served as an active trustee). Beyond the challenges of expanding mission, strategic planning, and policy governance are suggestions for significant modifications for boards and their presidents with regard to decision making, role clarity, and accountability.

Moving from the historical to the practical, the next three chapters look at organizational and operational aspects of governance. In Chapter Three, attorney Timothy K. Garfield discusses the challenges in managing a community college where the faculty are unionized. Unionization always results in some degree of power being shifted to the faculty, and governance becomes more legalistic as the provisions of collective bargaining contracts are added to the laws and policies of colleges. This chapter analyzes the major challenges of governing a community college with a unionized faculty and offers suggestions for dealing with these issues.

In Chapter Four, authors Michael T. Miller and Jennifer M. Miles describe the various approaches to internal shared governance utilized by community colleges, ranging from those that are intentional in their involvement of different constituent groups to those that evolve from habit, tradition, and precedence. Particular attention is given to how students, faculty (full- and part-time), and staff are involved and how external pressures affect these groups in efforts to influence decision making.

External influences on governance are discussed as part of the community colleges' workforce development imperative in Chapter Five. Here, Janice Nahra Friedel uses Kentucky and Iowa as case studies to explore the relationship between workforce development and community college governance. Kentucky's governor has called for higher education reform legislation through the creation of a new community college governance structure designed to create a responsive workforce development system. In Iowa, the legislature mandated a study of the locally governed system of community colleges, which reaffirmed a structure balancing local autonomy and state coordination to advance economic development and workforce development agendas.

In Chapter Six, Laurie Bricker, a member of the Texas Higher Education Coordinating Board and former president of the Board of the Houston Independent School District, outlines the development of P–16 initiatives in Texas and the impact of these initiatives on community college governance. This chapter also discusses the tension between local and state governance structures that arises in P–16 and P–20 environments.

NEW DIRECTIONS FOR COMMUNITY COLLEGES • DOI: 10.1002/cc

In Chapter Seven, John S. Levin discusses how community college governance varies not only regionally within the United States, but also across
international borders. The chapter offers a three-nation perspective on college governance, emphasizing the condition of autonomy embedded in governance arrangements.

Chapter Eight looks to the future, as Richard L. Alfred notes the lag
between rapidly changing forces in the external environment and static
capabilities within community colleges mandating transformation in organizational structures, systems, and governance. A governance model that
enables sustained growth and vitality is compared with more traditional
models in place in many community colleges. The chapter also examines
conditions inside colleges that fuel current models and identifies gaps
between "what is" and "what needs to be" to succeed in tomorrow's market.
It closes with recommendations for change in governance that will facilitate
colleges' success in a volatile environment. Finally, Chapter Nine, written
by Pam Schuetz, includes current resources that will be helpful to scholars
and practitioners seeking new directions for community college governance.

Robert C. Cloud
Susan T. Kater
Editors

References

Alfred, R. L., and Carter, P. "New Colleges for a New Century: Organizational Change and
    Development in Community Colleges." In J. C. Smart and W. G. Tierney (eds.), *Higher
    Education: Handbook of Theory and Research*, vol. XIV. New York: Agathon Press, 1999.
Amey, M. "Learning Leadership in Today's Community Colleges." *Community College
    Journal*, 2004, 74(4), 6–9.
Benjamin, R., and Carroll, S. "The Implications of the Changed Environment for Gov-
    ernance in Higher Education." In W. G. Tierney (ed.), *The Responsive University*. Bal-
    timore, Md.: Johns Hopkins University Press, 1998.
Davis, G. *Issues in Community College Governance*. Washington, D.C.: American Associ-
    ation of Community Colleges, 2000.
Ehrenberg, R. G. (ed.). *Governing Academia*. Ithaca, N.Y.: Cornell University Press, 2004.
Hines, E. R. "The Governance of Higher Education." In J. C. Smart and W. G. Tierney
    (eds.), *Higher Education: Handbook of Theory and Research*, vol. XV. New York:
    Agathon Press, 2000.
Pusser, B., Slaughter, S., and Thomas, S. L. "Playing the Board Game: An Empirical
    Analysis of University Trustee and Corporate Board Interlocks." *The Journal of Higher
    Education*, 2006, 77(5), 747–775.
Tierney, W. G. (ed.). *Competing Conceptions of Academic Governance: Negotiating the Per-
    fect Storm*. Baltimore, Md.: Johns Hopkins University Press, 2004.

ROBERT C. CLOUD *is professor of higher education at Baylor University.*

SUSAN T. KATER *is director of institutional planning, research, and effectiveness
at GateWay Community College in Phoenix, Arizona.*

1

This chapter sets the stage for understanding the
importance of governance in the community college.

Community College Governance: What Matters and Why?

Marilyn J. Amey, Eric Jessup-Anger, Jody Jessup-Anger

From rural Wisconsin to urban Miami, postsecondary education is facing increased scrutiny. Colleges and universities are responding to calls for transparency while reacting to substantial cuts in appropriations. Coupled with these mounting pressures are rising expectations from industry, government, and the public to increase the number of graduates and improve the quality of their educational experience. Institutional leaders are expected to do more with less while documenting the process for everyone to see.

Community colleges are among the most responsive of all postsecondary education institutions to societal change (Duderstadt, 2000). They have strong ties to local industry and government and play a role in promoting regional economic development. Consequently, community college leaders are on the front lines navigating the volatile terrain ahead for postsecondary education. This chapter will explore community college governance in a wider societal context, detailing external and internal factors that affect it. In addition, we discuss what matters about community college governance and raise a number of questions about the roles of various governance groups and structures. Finally, we explore the roles of different institutional leaders and the variation within governance models and processes.

Why Is Governance Important?

Before discussing the importance of community college governance, it is critical to define the concept. The term *governance* often refers to the structure and process of decision making a college uses to address internal and

external issues (Cohen and Brawer, 2003; Gayle, Tewarie, and White Jr., 2003; Levin, 1998). Governance takes many forms and involves several constituent groups, including faculty, administrators, trustees, union representatives, and students. Definitions of governance also need to encompass relationships between a college and the other entities it interacts with, including business, government, and community (Marginson and Considine, 2000). These myriad structures are often historical and a function of single or multicampus colleges or community college districts or other political entities. Community college governance parallels antecedents of university governance structures, but may be more influenced by the traditions of public school governance within a local or state setting because of the close historical links to schools during the junior college movement (Cohen and Brawer, 2003).

The comprehensive community college of the twenty-first century offers a full assortment of credit, non-credit, and lifelong learning experiences across a seemingly endless array of disciplines and technical curricula. With ever-growing organizational complexity, the internal and external environmental presses cannot go forever unmanaged; consequently, effective governance is increasingly important to organizational functioning (Amey and VanDerLinden, 2002). Gayle, Tewarie, and White Jr. (2003) note that "effective governance provides institutional purpose, clarifies strategic direction, identifies priorities, and exerts sufficient control to manage outcomes" (p. 1). It also facilitates institutional change and growth or, when ineffective, can lead to institutional decline.

Factors Affecting Community College Governance

Many factors affect governance structures and processes. Identifying a clear and operational mission when demands and expectations compete with one another is one significant force. Other forces include conflicting organizational goals, federal and state legislation, funding, judicial involvement, a resurgence in faculty participation, public scrutiny, local politics, community needs, cost containment, accountability, compliance mandates, changing student markets, competition, performance funding, attitudes and values of key decision makers, institutional culture, and board members (Amey, 2005; Amey and VanDerLinden, 2002; Levin, 1998). This complicated web of factors and forces is a challenge to manage and is not always understood by those charged with advancing the college's agenda (Davis, 2001). Yet it has never been more important for college administrators to grasp the fundamental aspects of governance and to lead effectively through them. Although each institution faces unique obstacles and opportunities because of its locale, we situate community college governance first in the national context in which college leaders find themselves and then address more institutional-level contexts.

True for all postsecondary institutions, and perhaps particularly for public community colleges, external agents increasingly act as catalysts for organizational change (Levin, 1998) and exert influence on college governance. Whereas external forces are common to almost all colleges and universities, some affect community colleges more strongly. Common external issues identified by community college leaders include financial support from local, state, and federal sources; K–12 student preparation; articulation agreements between high schools and other college and universities; community needs; links to business and industry; and other accountability and planning issues (Amey and VanDerLinden, 2002). Increased globalization, competition from for-profit and online service providers, and accreditation standards could easily be added to the list. Many of these issues are directly tied to federal, state, or institutional policies in which trustees, college presidents, and other participants in governance are directly involved.

The shifting expectations of federal and state entities have the potential to affect community college governance by issuing mandates and passing laws that may influence and realign priorities set by community college leaders. The U.S. Department of Education's (2006) report *A Test of Leadership: Charting the Future of U.S. Higher Education* is an example of the potential influence on community college governance. The report specifically addresses access, affordability, accountability, and quality in postsecondary education and recommends that institutions provide greater mobility within the higher education system and promote new learning paradigms for a broader range of students. If adopted, the report's recommendations require community college governance to review existing policies, processes, and relationships with other educational service providers. Although community colleges are historically sites of first entry for diverse learners (Cohen and Brawer, 2003; Horn and Nevill, 2006; Laden, 2004), more and different links may be needed to enable students to coordinate transfer, reverse transfer, and other fluid learning arrangements. Different kinds of articulation and tuition agreements, data management systems, joint programs, and degree sharing are just a few of the issues community colleges leaders may face if they hope to meet federal and state mandates and public expectations for meeting learner needs.

At the state level, blue-ribbon commissions and various legislative review committees have examined the status of educational systems as they connect to labor market and economic futures. In Michigan, the Cherry Commission's (2004) *Final Report of the Lt. Governor's Commission on Higher Education and the Economy* calls for increased access to higher education and training opportunities in order to jump-start the state economy. The report is congruent with Friedman's (2005) assessment that the changes currently influencing the economic outlook of the United States necessitate a dramatic reinvestment in the education of the workforce to drive domestic innovation and growth.

NEW DIRECTIONS FOR COMMUNITY COLLEGES • DOI: 10.1002/cc

In calling for students to be educated for a different and more demanding labor market, knowledge becomes central to new economic growth and development. As a result of this mandate, K-16 collaborative partnerships for seamless student learning are strongly encouraged (Amey, Eddy, and Ozaki, 2007; Boswell, 2000; Bragg, 2000). Similarly, partnerships between community colleges and various work settings have been called for, with policies and potential funding opportunities tied closely to the development of strong, effective collaborations (Orr and Bragg, 2001). However, as Orr and Bragg have also found, these partnerships are not always easy to establish and maintain. It is important for those involved in community college governance to understand the factors that contribute to success or failure of these collaborations, including differences in governance structures and processes between partnering organizations (Amey, Eddy, and Ozaki, 2007). In this way, leaders can determine how to best manage multiple demands on resources and remain responsive to the needs of constituent groups without inadvertently becoming the academic refuge for unfunded mandates and educational initiatives for which others do not want responsibility.

Underlying the discussion of federal and state reports is the reality that community colleges are faced with increased costs and decreased support from many traditional sources. Federal and state support for all of higher education is declining, and local funding is shrinking in deference to public school costs. Though still priced more reasonably than other forms of higher education, community colleges have been forced to pass rising costs along to students in the forms of tuition increases and various fee-for-service costs. As a result, the growing importance of financial aid requires community college leaders to be alert to legislation that affects their institutions.

Much federal funding provided to community colleges comes through student financial aid. Increasingly financial aid policies have data-collecting, reporting requirements, and accountability outcomes attached in order to retain funds (Lovell, 2001). Therefore, each time the government considers reauthorizing the Higher Education Act, Pell Grants, the Perkins Loan Program, or other forms of student financial aid, American Association of Community Colleges (AACC) representatives, Association of Community College Trustee members, and community college administrators actively engage in the debate (Lovell, 2001). How to obtain needed external dollars and to manage the complex accounting systems are skills required of effective administrators and senior leaders. Support for these efforts require that presidents and trustees cultivate strong relationships with state and federal legislators. Complacency and ignorance are unacceptable among governance leaders; coordination and collaboration across community colleges often increase leverage to acquire resources and stave off undue external political pressures.

Community colleges have historically assumed a significant role in workforce training, especially in occupational fields, just-in-time training, and high-need fields (Doughtery, 2001; Grubb, 1996). With the increased emphasis on education of the adult workforce as essential to a successful economy (Friedman, 2005; National Center for Public Policy and Higher Education, 2005), it is vital that community college leaders play a central role in expanding the development of opportunities for lifelong education—including meeting the rising demand for remedial and developmental coursework. Quality governance will regularly assess the cultivation of new programs and innovative curricular offerings that meet emerging local workforce needs with a commitment to maintaining a balanced and diversified institutional mission.

Workforce training resources continue to come through the Workforce Investment Act, the Carl Perkins Vocational and Technical Education Act of 1998 (Lovell, 2001), Tech Prep and Goals 2000 (Orr and Bragg, 2001), and other federal and state legislation and earmarked funding. As external funds supporting workforce training ebb and flow, and demand regularly exceeds funding levels, finding the balance of competing curricular needs and the resources and relationships to support them are continued challenges for governance leaders. Community college administrators, faculty, and trustees must understand national and local workforce trends and be prepared to guide collaborative institutional decision-making processes without alienating various constituencies when multiple missions and priorities are vying for limited resources. Successful community college leaders must be advocates for their institutions during the legislative process and savvy entrepreneurs without losing sight of their commitment to a comprehensive mission.

In addition to the aforementioned external forces, those involved in community college governance also have a number of internal factors with which to contend. As was true in our discussion of external influences, these internal pressures are not unique to community colleges, but their importance may be heightened and their resolution more complicated than similar factors at four-year institutions. When asked which internal issues were important to their institution, a national sample of community college presidents indicated that student retention, creation of new program delivery systems such as online instruction, technological support for instruction and administrative processes, student recruitment and marketing, and fiscal management and resource allocation were of greatest importance. They also expressed concern about governance issues such as board relations; and student development issues such as diversity, multiculturalism, and learning needs (Amey and VanDerLinden, 2002). Presidents did not expect these factors to dissipate or the college's mission to change in the future. But they did suggest that different strategies would be needed to achieve the mission, perhaps by implementing new pedagogies to meet changing student needs.

Another internal issue affecting governance structures and procedures is the faculty labor market, which includes a growing percentage of part-time staff (Cataldi, Fahimi, and Bradburn, 2005). Part-time faculty do not often participate in governance because of their diminished connection to campus or their status in unions or collective bargaining units. Nonetheless, part-time faculty members are not necessarily transient but often long-term employees of the college. Accordingly, there need to be ways of finding appropriate representation for them in institutional governance (Townsend and Twombly, 2007).

The factors discussed above, along with many others, demand the attention of community college leaders. With the rise of competing expectations facing community colleges, these factors affect how community college governance is structured, who is involved, and what processes help with effective decision making.

Considerations for Governance

If community colleges are to meet the rising and conflicting expectations of their multiple constituencies in an era of increasing external and internal pressures, they will need highly effective governance and leadership to guide them. Effective governance is defined as the structure and processes that achieve desired outcomes via a decision-making process grounded in thoughtful deliberation and evidence. However, critics of institutional governance from both inside and outside academe argue that it is rarely effective. Dimond (1991) found that 70 percent of administrators, faculty, and staff perceived the decision-making process at their institution as ineffective and laborious. Birnbaum (2000) poked fun at postsecondary institutions' pursuit of management fads. In his analysis he highlighted the numerous structural and process changes that rarely led to the intended improvements in effectiveness or efficiency. Still, when leaders determine that change is needed, the structure of governance is often the first thing to be examined and adjusted.

Echoing Birnbaum's criticisms, Kezar (2004) explains that "there is widespread acknowledgement of the governance problem, but few solutions have been proposed and, of those, few have proven successful" (p. 35). She posited that one reason for the governance problem might be the historical focus on the effectiveness of governance structures rather than on the role of other processes such as culture, communication, preparation, and team-based leadership. This longstanding trend appears to be shifting. Kaplan (2004) recently found that "outcomes in higher education may be more significantly related to factors beyond structural arrangements" (p. 32). He noted that institutional culture might play a significant role, along with the wider environment in which governance issues are embedded. Other recent studies of various administrative, leadership, and governance issues have also found that factors such as culture, trust, involvement, and sense making affect effectiveness as much as structures (Amey, 2005; Pope and Miller, 2005; Pope, 2004). These findings suggest an awareness of the growing importance of context related to institutional governance.

How communication occurs within and between institutional governance structures and constituents is also of great importance. The involvement of faculty in community college governance, particularly through faculty senates, is often sporadic, especially as the percentage of part-time and adjunct instructors increases. Yet faculty can provide useful input into a broad array of institutional issues and act as an effective sounding board for administrators and trustees (Pope, 2003). Tierney and Minor (2004) emphasize the need for effective communication in faculty governance, concluding that faculty must understand institutional communication strategies as well as structural reforms if they are to be more effective in contributing to the college's mission. Kezar's (2004) review of governance case studies showed that "leadership, trust, and relationships supersede structures and processes in effective decision making" (p. 44). She closed by stating that "campuses can build effective governance through an investment in leadership development and through mechanisms that nurture faculty, staff, and administrative relationships" (p. 45).

Although preparing those involved in community college governance is an often stated priority, the challenge to do so seems never ending, in part because of the continuous leadership turnover among presidents and board members. In reviewing issues affecting the quality of community college governance, Davis (2001) concluded that the lack of a complex understanding of institutional issues among many trustees was a significant detriment to their ability to effectively meet the needs of constituent groups. Institutions that fail to orient their trustees or provide them with sufficient information to understand key issues decrease the likelihood of highly effective governance.

The similar lack of preparation for administrative leaders and the question of an adequate pool of well-trained future leaders has been a particular concern over the last several years (Amey and VanDerLinden, 2002; Schults, 2001). This problem is exacerbated by the growing retirements among a generation of community college presidents and their most senior administrative colleagues. This perceived leadership vacuum is worsened by the lack of institutionally based or national programs designed to prepare midlevel community college administrators for successful transitions into presidential positions. Vaughan and Weisman (2003) recommend the development of programs jointly developed by a president and board team to prepare future community college leaders, and there is some movement in this direction at both state and national levels, such as the League for Innovation in Community Colleges and the Michigan Community College Association. In addition, AACC's Leading Forward project showcased Grow Your Own programs (Jeandron, 2006) and cutting-edge graduate programs (Amey, 2006), as well as its own Leadership Competencies as emerging strategies for adequately preparing current and future leaders to face the challenges of the twenty-first-century comprehensive community college.

As those responsible for institutional governance face increasingly complex issues with fewer experienced leaders to guide their institutions, team-based leadership may provide some solutions to a number of pressing governance challenges. Bensimon and Neumann (1993) examined the role of leadership teams and concluded that although they are not without challenges, team-based leadership is promising practice. They found that effective use of teams increased the complexity of analysis and the quality and creativity of problem solving and decision making. Consensus building and gathering input from various constituents, which are hallmarks of team leadership, improve governance processes (Evans, 1999) and are consistent with the culture of shared governance prevalent at many community colleges. In addition, team-based leadership often encourages midlevel leaders to develop skills, attitudes, and perspectives essential for their development as institutional leaders.

Conclusion

The organizational context for community college governance is growing more complex. Community college administrators, faculty, and trustees must meet the challenge of sustaining a comprehensive mission under which most colleges were founded while also making difficult choices between often competing areas of emphasis in times of economic instability. Compounding these challenges are internal and external factors that demand increasing amounts of leaders' attention. It is clear that those involved in community college governance need to be well informed about federal, state, and institutional issues and policies. In addition, they need to be well versed in politics and policies surrounding labor markets, funding sources, revenue streams, community agendas, and student learning needs. Perhaps most importantly, they need to acknowledge the unique organizational features and roles of community colleges in the P–20 educational system and be prepared to develop the necessary governance structures and processes that best achieve the goals of this sector.

References

Amey, M. J. "Leadership as Learning: Conceptualizing the Process." *Community College Journal of Research and Practice*, 2005, 29(9), 689–704.

Amey, M. J. *Breaking Tradition: New Community College Leadership Programs Meet 21st Century Needs*. Washington, D.C.: American Association of Community Colleges, 2006.

Amey, M. J., and VanDerLinden, K. E. *The Institutional Context of Community College Administration*. Washington, D.C.: American Association of Community Colleges, 2002.

Amey, M. J., Eddy, P., and Ozaki, C. "Demands for Partnership and Collaboration in Higher Education: A Model." In M. J. Amey (ed.), *Collaborations Across Educational Sectors*. New Directions for Community Colleges, no. 139. San Francisco: Jossey-Bass, 2007.

Bensimon, E. M., and Neumann, A. *Redesigning Collegiate Leadership*. Baltimore, Md.: Johns Hopkins University Press, 1993.

Birnbaum, R. *Management Fads in Higher Education*. San Francisco: Jossey-Bass, 2000.

Boswell, K. "Building Bridges or Barriers? Public Policies That Facilitate or Impede Linkages Between Community Colleges and Local School Districts." In J. C. Palmer (ed.), *How Community Colleges Can Create Productive Collaborations with Local*

Schools. New Directions for Community Colleges, no. 111. San Francisco: Jossey-Bass, 2000.

Bragg, D. D. "Maximizing the Benefits of Tech-Prep Initiatives for High School Students." In J. C. Palmer (ed.), *How Community Colleges Can Create Productive Collaborations with Local Schools.* New Directions for Community Colleges, no. 111. San Francisco: Jossey-Bass, 2000.

Cataldi, E., Fahimi, M., and Bradburn, E. M. *National Study of Postsecondary Faculty Report on Faculty and Instructional Staff in Fall 2003.* Washington, D.C.: U.S. Department of Education, 2005.

Cherry Commission. *Final Report of the Lt. Governor's Commission on Higher Education and Economic Growth.* Lansing: Michigan Department of Education, 2004.

Cohen, A. M., and Brawer, F. B. *The American Community College.* (4th ed.) San Francisco: Jossey-Bass, 2003.

Davis, G. *Issues in Community College Governance.* Washington, D.C.: American Association of Community Colleges and Association of Community College Trustees, 2001. www.aacc.nche.edu/Content/NavigationMenu/ResourceCenter/Projects_Partnerships/Current/NewExpeditions/IssuePapers/Issues_in_CC_Governance.htm. Accessed Nov. 1, 2007.

Dimond, J. "Faculty Participation in Institutional Budgeting." In R. Birnbaum (ed.), *Faculty in Governance: The Role of Senates and Joint Committees in Academic Decision Making.* New Directions for Higher Education, no. 75. San Francisco: Jossey-Bass, 1991.

Doughtery, K. J. "State Policies and the Community College's Role in Workforce Preparation." In B. Townsend and S. B. Twombly (eds.), *Community Colleges: Policy in the Future Context.* Westport, Conn.: Ablex, 2001.

Duderstadt, J. J. *A University for the 21st Century.* Ann Arbor: University of Michigan Press, 2000.

Evans, J. P. "Benefits and Barriers to Shared Authority." In M. Miller (ed.), *Responsive Academic Decision Making Involving Faculty in Higher Education Governance.* Stillwater, Okla.: New Forums, 1999.

Friedman, T. *The World Is Flat: A Brief History of the 21st Century.* New York: Farrar, Straus, and Giroux, 2005.

Gayle, D. J., Tewarie, B., and White, Jr., A. Q. *Governance in the Twenty-First Century University: Approaches to Effective Leadership and Strategic Management.* ASHE Higher Education Report, no. 30. San Francisco: Jossey-Bass, 2003.

Grubb, W. N. *Working in the Middle.* San Francisco: Jossey-Bass, 1996.

Horn, L. J., and Nevill, S. *Profile of Undergraduates in U.S. Postsecondary Education Institutions: 2003–04, with a Special Analysis of Community College Students.* Washington, D.C.: U.S. Department of Education, 2006.

Jeandron, C. *Growing Your Own Leaders: Community Colleges Step Up.* Washington, D.C.: American Association of Community Colleges, 2006.

Kaplan, G. E. "Do Governance Structures Matter?" In W. G. Tierney and V. M. Lachuga (eds.), *Restructuring Shared Governance in Higher Education.* New Directions for Higher Education, no. 127. San Francisco: Jossey-Bass, 2004.

Kezar, A. "What Is More Effective Governance: Relationships, Trust, and Leadership or Structures and Formal Processes?" In W. G. Tierney and V. M. Lachuga (eds.), *Restructuring Shared Governance in Higher Education.* New Directions for Higher Education, no. 127. San Francisco: Jossey-Bass, 2004.

Laden, B. V. "Serving Emerging Majority Students." In B. V. Laden (ed.), *Serving Minority Populations.* New Directions for Community Colleges, no. 127. San Francisco: Jossey-Bass, 2004.

Levin, J. S. "Making Sense of Organizational Change." In J. S. Levin (ed.), *Organizational Change and the Community College.* New Directions for Community Colleges, no. 102. San Francisco: Jossey-Bass, 1998.

Lovell, C. D. "Federal Policies and Community Colleges: A Mix of Federal and Local Influences." In B. Townsend and S. B. Twombly (eds.), *Community Colleges: Policy in the Future Context*. Westport, Conn.: Ablex, 2001.

Marginson, S., and Considine, M. *The Enterprise University: Power, Governance and Reinvention in Australia*. New York: Cambridge University Press, 2000.

National Center for Public Policy and Higher Education. *Income of U.S. Workforce Projected to Decline if Education Doesn't Improve*. Washington, D.C.: National Center for Public Policy and Higher Education, 2005.

Orr, M. T., and Bragg, D. D. "Policy Directions for K-14 Education: Looking to the Future." In B. K. Townsend and S. B. Twombly (eds.), *Community Colleges: Policy in the Future Context*. Westport, Conn.: Ablex, 2001.

Pope, M. L. "Faculty Governance in Community Colleges: A Distinct Perspective on Broad-Based Decision Making." In M. Miller and J. Caplow (eds.), *Policy and University Faculty Governance*. Greenwich, Conn.: Information Age, 2003.

Pope, M. L. "A Conceptual Framework of Faculty Trust and Participation in Governance." In W. G. Tierney and V. M. Lechuga (eds.), *Restructuring Shared Governance in Higher Education*. New Directions for Higher Education, no. 127. San Francisco: Jossey-Bass, 2004.

Pope, M. L., and Miller, M. T. "Leading from the Inside Out: Learned Respect for Academic Culture Through Shared Governance." *Community College Journal of Research and Practice*, 2005, 29(9), 745–756.

Schults, C. *The Critical Impact of Impending Retirements on Community College Leadership*. Research Brief. Washington, D.C.: American Association of Community Colleges, 2001.

Tierney, W. G., and Minor, J. T. "A Cultural Perspective on Communication and Governance." In W. G. Tierney and V. M. Lachuga (eds.), *Restructuring Shared Governance in Higher Education*. New Directions for Higher Education, no. 127. San Francisco: Jossey-Bass, 2004.

Townsend, B., and Twombly, S. B. *Community College Faculty: Overlooked and Undervalued*. ASHE Higher Education Report, no. 32. San Francisco: Jossey-Bass, 2007.

U.S. Department of Education. *A Test of Leadership: Charting the Future of U.S. Higher Education*. Washington, D.C.: U.S. Department of Education, 2006.

Vaughan, G. B., and Weisman, I. M. "Leadership Development: The Role of the President-Board Team." In W. E. Piland and D. B. Wolf (eds.), *Help Wanted: Preparing Community College Leaders in a New Century*. New Directions for Community Colleges, no. 123. San Francisco: Jossey-Bass, 2003.

MARILYN J. AMEY *is professor and chair of the Department of Educational Administration at Michigan State University.*

ERIC JESSUP-ANGER *is a graduate research assistant in the Higher, Adult, and Lifelong Education program in the College of Education at Michigan State University.*

JODY JESSUP-ANGER *is a graduate research assistant in the Higher, Adult, and Lifelong Education program in the College of Education at Michigan State University.*

This chapter provides an overview of board governance, its effectiveness, and changes over more than four decades. The authors also offer strategies for creating partnerships between presidents and trustees that lead to future institutional success.

Governance over the Years: A Trustee's Perspective

George E. Potter, Daniel J. Phelan

The publication of John Carver's (1997) book *Boards That Make a Difference* should have served as a wake-up call for community college boards across the country. Unfortunately, it has not captured their collective attention. Early on, the leadership of the Association of Community College Trustees (ACCT) recognized the importance of policy governance and Carver's governance model. ACCT subsequently brought Carver to its annual meeting to make a presentation to the attendees and employed facilitators to assist boards in implementing the new model (Carver, 1999). ACCT went so far as to contract with Carver and his associate, Miriam Mayhew, to write a second book titled *A New Vision of Board Leadership: Governing the Community College* (Carver and Mayhew, 1994). Still, only modest attention was given to this new methodology.

Unfortunately, only about 15 percent of community and technical college boards adopted this policy governance model. Some boards failed to consider the Carver model because it represented a change from the comfortable status quo. Others embraced the practice but have since abandoned it either because the trustees failed to effectively implement the model or because some of the trustees did not like the loss of control over decisions made by the president or chancellor.

Historical Considerations

At the start of the twentieth century, some community colleges were created as junior college departments of public school districts, and local school boards governed them. Historically school boards have used, and continue

to employ, the approval model when governing. They have traditionally viewed their role as that of watchdog for the public interest, particularly, but not exclusively, in financial matters. In an attempt to ensure that the college did not hire persons improperly, spend money unwisely, or take inappropriate action, the board insisted on approving all significant administrative decisions.

In the 1950s and 1960s, a number of legislative acts were passed that permitted the establishment of community and technical colleges with their own governing boards. Frequently, however, the trustees elected or appointed to those boards had previously served as school board members. Thus, they brought with them the governance philosophy and methods they were accustomed to as school board members.

School boards, then and now, spend most of their meetings approving the expenditure of funds and the hiring of personnel. Nothing that occurs in the school district escapes their attention if they can help it. Bus routes, school lunch menus, curriculum changes, instructional equipment purchases, textbooks used, and nearly everything else in school operations has been the subject of review, debate, and decision by school boards.

Even for those new college trustees who had not themselves served on a school board, the closest model available was the local school board. Consequently, most community college boards adopted the approval model for governance of their institutions. This meeting format left little time for the board leadership to establish a clear mission, create a vision for direction, or set goals or outcomes. For most boards their activities entailed approving the mission, vision statements, and goals developed by the administration.

Community college boards did, however, understand they were responsible for establishing policy for their institutions. After all, school boards had been adopting policies for their school districts for decades. In typical school district form, board policies were established for almost every conceivable issue that might arise at the college. Some policies emerged because of problems with an individual employee or reflected the desire of a particular board member. In most cases it is not uncommon for community college board policy manuals to consist of hundreds of pages directing the staff what to do, when to do it, and how to do it.

The approval model worked, though not always well, for the first century of public two-year colleges in the United States. However, there were many college superintendents, presidents, trustees, and governance experts who urged boards to abandon their watchdog role and provide a meaningful leadership role. Indeed, principles of effective governance were well known and advocated by many. Unfortunately, some boards found it difficult to give up their traditional role and thus the approval model continues to dominate the community college landscape today.

In an effort to moderate some of the limitations associated with the traditional approach to board governance, John Carver (1997) took the principles of effective governance and created a model that challenged the board to fulfill its leadership role and abandon the approval model of governance. As Carver stated, "moving mountains an inch often appears less active than moving mole hills a mile. Boards who would be strategic leaders must move at a more deliberate pace than their staffs, but with issues far more momentous" (Carver, 1997, p. 196). Still, unique actions such as constructing a new building, buying land, or purchasing expensive equipment continue to require board approval, even under the new approach.

Basic Principles of Effective Board Governance

Carver's (1997) policy governance approach is driven by a number of unique aspects that are essential to ensure efficient operations of the college while preserving the vital leadership role of the board. The following list enumerates those essential principles derived from actual practice at Jackson Community College in Jackson, Michigan.

The Board Is Principally Involved in Deciding Ends. Ends are the board's desired outcomes for the college, as opposed to *means,* the operations needed to achieve those goals. Thus, the creation of institutional goals, both short- and long-term, is a critical board responsibility. This does not imply that the board merely rubber-stamps goals brought to it by the president. Rather, the board should gather input from all appropriate sources (the president, staff, students, and community) and work jointly with the president to develop the institutional goals. While staff, division, and department goals are the responsibility of the staff, it is the president who is responsible for ensuring that those goals are consistent with the board's institutional goals.

Ends also include establishing the college's mission statement and basic objectives of the college. *Ends* should address the following types of questions: Is the college to be a comprehensive community college, or is it to serve a more limited role by providing only transfer or technical education? Is the college going to offer customized job training? Is the college going to operate a museum or nature center? Is the college going to offer cultural programs for the community? Answering these and other similar questions is the responsibility of the board.

The Board Should Focus Primarily on the Future. Unfortunately, most boards spend their time reverting to the approval model by reviewing the past or making decisions for the present (the hiring of an administrator or purchasing of a piece of equipment), rather than planning for the future. With the rapid changes in technology, the erosion of state and local tax support, changing student demographics, and the transition to an information-based economy, boards must devote much more time to preparing for the future. Boards must be responsible for establishing a vision statement and a strategic plan that address such questions as, What is the college going to look like in ten years? How and to whom will instruction be delivered in the future? How will it be funded? Boards that fail to deal with these issues now will almost certainly find their colleges in serious trouble ten years down the road.

NEW DIRECTIONS FOR COMMUNITY COLLEGES • DOI: 10.1002/cc

Institutional Outcomes Are Measured by the College and Monitored by the Board. Regional accrediting bodies and other federal and state agencies require colleges to adopt institutional effectiveness measures. Even in the absence of outside agencies' mandates, effective boards have been insisting on monitoring effectiveness for several years. In fact, one of the authors of this article identified evaluating institutional performance as a board responsibility in the mid-1970s (Potter, 1976). Measurement, effectiveness evaluation, and monitoring by the board should seek answers to the following questions: Are student goals being met? Are transfer students doing well at the colleges or universities to which they have transferred? Are occupational students being employed in their occupational field of study upon graduation? Did the college prepare them well for their pursued occupation? Are the students and their employers satisfied with the skills they learned at the college? Effective boards do not require simply that institutional effectiveness measures be used by the college. Rather, they insist the results be reported to the board in a timely manner. Furthermore, the board requires the administration to set targets and to inform the board how it plans to address any unsatisfactory results.

The Board Acts Through Policies. Occasionally a board may need to make ad hoc decisions due to unique or significant issues. For example, approving the construction of a new building, approving the sale of property, and the hiring of a new president are all ad hoc decisions. However, effective governance occurs with the adoption of policies that provide guidance and direction to the administration on matters falling within the policy. Policies should set the priorities of the board and be strategic and manageable. Board policies should provide broad direction for the administration, not detailed instructions on how employees should do their jobs.

In his piece on governance, Carver (1997) stated:

> With respect to staff it is pivotal that the board not only lead, but lead leaders. Bigness must be passed on. Leading leaders calls for mentality that allows others to make decisions. The board should never give the message, by trying to intervene in every potential mistake, that to err is unacceptable. Emphasizing the avoidance of errors, rather than the creation of breakthroughs, propagates not leaders, but followers. It encourages not decision makers, but bureaucrats. Leading leaders calls for the tolerance of risk, for leaders do not remain in the same old ruts. They try and sometimes fail. One approach is to view governance as empowerment. The board passes power to others and expects them to use it as assertively and creatively as they dare [p. 199].

The Board Acts Only as a Whole. Board members individually have no power or authority to direct staff. Unfortunately there are many community college trustees who believe their election or appointment to office gave them the right to order the president and other members of the college staff to do something the trustee would personally like to see done. In fact, there is no state law that gives individual trustees the authority to direct any college employee to do anything. The legal vesting of power to instruct the staff occurs only when the full board acts at a valid meeting of the board. The full board may delegate to the board chair or another member of the board the authority to provide specific direction to the president or to take other action on the part of the board. However, this delegation should occur only on rare occasion and at a valid meeting of the full board.

A majority decision of the full board should be supported by all members of the board to the extent their consciences will permit. Rarely does a board decision justify dissenting board members withholding support for the decision. One of the hallmarks of truly effective boards is the acceptance, in almost every case of majority decisions, by those trustees who voted against the decision.

All Authority Delegated by the Board Is Delegated to the President. This seems obvious to most students of institutional management. However, occasionally boards will by policy or ad hoc decision delegate authority to other administrators. This interrupts the normal chain of command and allows the president to escape responsibility for the actions of the administrator to whom the board has delegated some authority. It clearly undermines the ability of the president to manage the college and is inappropriate.

The worst example of the delegation of authority to an administrator other than the president occurs when the board selects a person to be responsible directly to the board and requires the person to provide information regarding the operations of the college. This is often done when the majority of the board loses confidence in the president or no longer trusts the president to provide accurate and complete information. Instead of terminating the president, the board bypasses the president, causing the staff to lose confidence in the president and making it impossible for the president to manage. If the board has lost faith in its president, it is the members' responsibility to bring closure to the relationship.

The Board's Highest Priority Is Student Learning and Student Success. Unfortunately, the highest priority of most boards is often related to financial matters. With few exceptions, most boards spend at least 50 percent of their time at board meetings discussing and debating issues that involve money. Most trustees identify the sound fiscal operation of the college as their most important responsibility. Colleges were not established because the voters wanted to pay taxes to create a public agency that soundly managed its money. Certainly responsible fiscal operation of the college is expected by the voters and should be a priority of the board. However, most persons would agree community colleges were established to provide learning opportunities to students. Almost all comprehensive community and technical colleges were created to offer occupational training to residents, provide the first two years of a baccalaureate program, and support transfer to a four-year college or university. Therefore, it is reasonable to expect boards to make student success their highest priority.

NEW DIRECTIONS FOR COMMUNITY COLLEGES • DOI: 10.1002/cc

Beyond the aforementioned principles of policy governance, nothing is more important to the success of the college than the relationship between the board and the president. For a college to thrive, it generally requires a strong, skilled, ethical, and visionary board and a president working together as a team. It is always difficult for a president to provide effective future-oriented leadership for a college without the help and support of a good, effective board. Likewise, it is impossible for a board to lead the college forward successfully without a good president working with the board to set direction for the college, implement board policies, and direct the means to accomplish board ends. This strong relationship should be forged and established from the beginning.

Anderson (2003) rightly noted that the board should help the new president get off on the right foot through a number of activities that the board should manage. In addition to the ceremonial inauguration and standard introductions, she recommends board-facilitated meetings with legislators, locally elected officials, and other community leaders. As a consultant she noted how this approach clarified "the importance of these meetings and equipped [presidents] to maximize their impact by sharing their vision for the college and by discussing the perceived needs of the college"(p. 33). Additionally, there are a number of key operating practices that will ensure a successful and strong association over the subsequent years.

Principles of Good Board and President Relations

Clearly the board of trustees is responsible for the college. However, it must hire a chief executive officer to carry out the mission, advance the organization, and serve the needs of its constituency. Again, based on the practical experience of a long-serving trustee, the following basic principles, essential to a good board-president relationship, are offered below.

A Strong Sense of Trust Exists Between the President and Board. The board must feel confident that the president is honest and ethical, provides complete and timely information to the board, and always acts in the best interest of the college. Similarly, the president must feel confident the board members are honest and ethical, have no hidden agendas, and always speak and act in a manner that is consistent with the best interests of the college.

It is not enough for the president and trustees to tell each other the truth—they must not withhold information from each other. For example, a president making a recommendation to the board that contains only information supporting the recommendation and withholds relevant but unsupportive information will cause erosion of the board's trust. This is particularly true if the board adopts the recommendation and a problem that was foreseeable by the president occurs later. Former trustee Vaughn Sherman stated: "Yet, it is hard to think of a single matter more critical to good board-president relations than being able to rely on the complete integrity of each board member, the board as a whole and the president" (2000, p. 1).

The President Treats Board Members Equally. Once an individual board member is given information by the president, then all board members should receive the same information (Smith, 2000). On rare occasions, the president may share information with the board chair that for a valid reason may be kept private for a few days. Ultimately, though, sharing information with all board members in a timely manner is absolutely vital. The same caveat applies to the board chair. The chair must share the same information with all board members.

Open and Appropriate Communication Exists Between the President and Board. Keeping all board members informed must be a high priority for the president. No board member likes to hear something about the college, a college employee, or student from someone outside the college or from the news media. Private matters involving a college employee or student are no longer private if they are likely to be disclosed by the news media or are commonly known by those on campus. Nothing is more embarrassing to a trustee than to hear from someone outside the college about a significant event that occurred at the college.

The President and Board Respect Each Other's Right to Make Decisions. If the president makes an administrative decision, board members should respect the president's right to make the decision and should support the decision, even if one or more board members disagree with it. Likewise the president must respect and accept decisions made by the board on policy matters, institutional goals, or other matters that are within the purview of the board's decision-making responsibility.

The Board Never Undermines the President's Authority. If the board members have lost confidence in their institutional leader, the appropriate action for the board to take is to replace the president. However, undermining the president's authority, stripping the president of adequate authority to manage the college, or delegating administrative authority to other employees causes serious harm to the institution. Such actions are more harmful in the long run than replacing a president in whom the board no longer has confidence.

The Board Evaluates the President Annually. This approach to performance review accomplishes two objectives. First, it is essential the president know he or she is on the same wavelength as the board and is managing the college in accordance with the board's expectations. Second, the evaluation should be used to improve the president's performance (Smith, 2000). The basis of the president's evaluation should focus primarily on the accomplishment of the board's ends, the institutional strategic plan, and outcomes policies and annual goals established by the board. The board and the president should agree in advance on the points of evaluation and the method of evaluation.

The Board Protects the President, and the President Protects the Board. Each should constantly be on the lookout for a problem that could embarrass the other. Each should help the other avoid situations or actions that could make it difficult for the other to carry out his or her responsibilities. There should be no surprises. Board members should not bring up something at a public board meeting that is a surprise to the president and his or her fellow trustees. Likewise, presidents normally should not bring something up at a public board meeting that is a surprise to the board members.

The Board and President Recognize They Are a Team. While boards should give significant authority to the president to manage the institution, the president needs to recognize it is not always wise to exercise that authority without board input or knowledge. For example, if the president has authority to hire and fire other administrators, the executive may find it in his or her best interest to seek informal concurrence of the board on certain decisions. For example, firing a popular administrator without first informing the board members of the intention and the reasons for doing so could result in a serious problem for the president and the college, particularly if a majority of the trustees express their opposition to the firing.

There is a significant benefit to presidents who minimally consult or seek informal approval of the board members regarding major presidential decisions. If the decision turns out to be wrong, it is difficult for boards to criticize the president for making the decision when the board members informally approved the decision or at least had an opportunity to advise against the decision and failed to do so. Boards almost always ask for input from the president before making decisions, even though the board has the unquestionable right to make the decision. Failure to follow the president's advice can become a disaster for the board and the college.

Rogue Trustees

One of the most frequently asked questions is how to deal with board members who engage in inappropriate behavior. These board members are frequently referred to as rogue trustees. Sometimes they are loners on the board; sometimes they are part of a rogue minority element on the board. When the rogue element becomes the board majority, the solution to the problem lies solely in the hands of the voters who elected them or the appointing authority that selected them. Obviously it is ideal to prevent prospective problem trustees from election or appointment to the board. Thus, existing board members have a duty to encourage good candidates to seek election or appointment to the board.

Developing a good training or orientation program for new board members can help prevent problem board members. The orientation must include training in board culture, familiarization with board policies and practices, and a thorough explanation of board ethical standards. Every board should have a policy in place prescribing ethical standards for the trustees.

However, when a problem trustee is elected or appointed to the board and an orientation program fails to improve the trustee's behavior, the board chair and other board members should meet with the problem trustee to discuss their concerns about his or her behavior. The best persons to assist in this task are those board members who are friends of the problem trustee. If no such relationship exists, then any board members who have the greatest respect within the community should approach the challenging trustee.

Should undesirable behavior continue after attempts at remediation, the majority of the board may be required to publicly reprimand or censure the rogue trustee. This should be accomplished only as a last resort, but a board should be willing to do so if the bad behavior continues and is having a harmful effect on the board's operations, the president's management of the college, or the college itself.

The arrival of a wayward trustee to a board can occur for many reasons. Some seek election or appointment to the board because they have an ax to grind. For example, the trustee's daughter may have been denied admission to the college's nursing program, or a close friend was terminated as college administrator, or they applied for a job at the college and were not hired, or they dislike the president. Still others represent a special interest group and are committed to advancing the cause of that group, even if it is not in the best interest of the college.

In some instances rogue board members may demonstrate an exaggerated use of personal power while serving on the board. Their behavior can include attempting to dominate discussion, going off on tangents unrelated to the subject under discussion, attacking the president or chair, or claiming to be an expert on the subject matter. Those rogue trustees whose behavior results from personal conflicts about their role on the board are most likely to improve. Involving those persons in board social events, getting them to participate in trustee training at state and national conferences, and going out of the way to make them feel part of the team may bring about a positive change in their behavior.

Summary

The changes community colleges face are enormous, to be sure. In the face of these challenges, the board must provide strong strategic leadership for the college. Boards must devote their energy to leading the college into a successful future. As Carver (1997) stated, "successful strategic leadership demands powerful engagement with trusteeship, obsessive concern over results, enthusiastic empowerment of people, bigness in embracing the farsighted view, and the commitment to take a stand for dreams of tomorrow's human condition" (p. 212). Likewise, CEOs must work for the best of the college strategically and operationally, an approach that ultimately leads to the success of students. Both the president and the board should approach their individual and collective responsibilities with integrity and in a deliberate, thoughtful, and purposeful manner.

References

Anderson, B. J. "A Strong Board Is Necessary to Select a Strong President." *Trustee Quarterly,* Fall 2003, p. 33.

Carver, J. *Boards That Make a Difference.* (2nd ed.) San Francisco: Jossey-Bass, 1997.

Carver, J. "Community College Governance." Paper presented at the annual meeting of the Association of Community College Trustees, Toronto, April 1999.

Carver, J., and Mayhew, M. *A New Vision of Board Leadership: Governing the Community College.* Washington, D.C.: Association of Community College Trustees, 1994.

Potter, G. E. "Responsibilities." In V. Dziuba and W. Meardy (eds.), *Enhancing Trustee Effectiveness.* New Directions for Community Colleges, no. 15. San Francisco: Jossey-Bass, 1976.

Sherman, V. *The Essentials of Board-CEO Relations.* Washington, D.C.: Association of Community College Trustees, 2000.

Smith, C. J. *Trusteeship in Community College: A Guide of Effective Governance.* Washington, D.C.: Association of Community College Trustees, 2000.

GEORGE E. POTTER is trustee emeritus, having served forty-four years as a trustee at Jackson Community College in Jackson, Michigan.

DANIEL J. PHELAN is president at Jackson Community College in Jackson, Michigan.

3

The presence of a faculty union in a community college has a significant impact on its governance. This chapter offers recommendations for dealing with the challenges presented by collective bargaining in the postsecondary education environment.

Governance in a Union Environment

Timothy K. Garfield

Managing a community college is not easy in the best of circumstances. Managing a community college whose faculty is represented by a union is considerably more challenging. Unionization always results in some degree of power being shifted to the faculty (Wollett, 1976), and governance becomes more cumbersome and legalistic. This chapter reviews the impact a faculty union has on governance, analyzes the major challenges presented by a unionized faculty, and offers suggestions for dealing with those challenges.

The governance structure of the typical community college is relatively simple. Overall responsibility for the college is legally vested in a governing board. The governing board selects a president (and a chancellor, in multi-campus districts) and other senior management officials. The board sets overall policy, and senior management carries out the policy and oversees the day-to-day operation of the college. Usually a faculty senate makes some decisions on instructional and curriculum issues, and faculty committees deal with academic policies and some operational issues. While the community college normally does not replicate the shared governance model of four-year institutions in which the faculty has a significant voice in the operation of the institution, the typical community college faculty does have substantial input into instructional and other academic decisions.

For purposes of this chapter, a union environment is one in which the faculty has voted to appoint an organization to be its exclusive representative in employer-employee relations. The faculty organization represents all members of the bargaining unit, whether or not they are actually members of the union itself. The exclusive representative is selected under, and operates

NEW DIRECTIONS FOR COMMUNITY COLLEGES, no. 141, Spring 2008 © 2008 Wiley Periodicals, Inc.
Published online in Wiley InterScience (www.interscience.wiley.com) • DOI: 10.1002/cc.312

pursuant to, state laws that regulate the relationship between the union and the college. Although these laws vary from state to state, they generally have a common basic structure, which will be briefly described in this chapter.

It should be noted that faculty members to some degree see themselves as the true management of their colleges. Faculty formulate significant policies concerning curriculum, graduation requirements, student conduct, professional standards such as qualifications for employment of new faculty members, and other critical standards for institutional operation. The bilateral labor-management dichotomy does not fully fit employer-employee relations in the typical public postsecondary institution, which is a blend of shared governance, substantial government regulations, and collective bargaining. The often adversarial negotiation process may not be well suited to faculty who view themselves as professionals, and collegial structures for shared governance are likely to be reduced in a unionized environment (Rapp, 2007).

Governance Structure in a Union Environment

The presence of an exclusive representative at a college in many cases adds an additional level to the decision-making process. The union itself becomes an important structure in governance, just like the governing board, management, and the academic senate. While the authority of the union is not all-encompassing, its authority is often substantial. Many decisions that are made solely by management and the board in a nonunion environment must first be negotiated with the exclusive representative in a union environment.

A faculty union normally enters the governance picture through a process established by law. As public institutions, community colleges are governed by the labor relations statutes of the state in which they are located, rather than by the federal National Labor Relations Act (NLRA), which applies to private institutions. Public postsecondary institutions in thirty-five states have some form of collective bargaining (Kaplin and Lee, 2006). The labor relations laws in these states vary widely but generally outline a unionization process that includes the following steps: a significant number of the faculty indicate, either by signing a petition or other show of support, that they desire to be represented by a specific employee organization as their exclusive representative. Unless the show of support includes a majority of the faculty in the proposed employee unit, an election is held at which employees of the proposed unit vote on whether they want the organization to be their exclusive representative. If a majority so indicates, the organization is selected as the exclusive representative of the unit, and management may not deal with other employee organizations concerning wages, hours, and other terms and conditions of employment of unit members. This definition of the scope of mandatory bargaining originated in the NLRA, and most states also use this definition or a close variation. The precise meaning of the concept of terms and conditions of employment varies from state to state, according to state law. The organization and the governing board then meet and negotiate on terms and conditions of employment such as salary, health and welfare benefits, hours of work, and other topics selected by the organization and the board. Once agreements are reached, a collective bargaining agreement is executed. The board is then legally bound to adhere to the bargained terms and conditions for the duration of the collective bargaining agreement. Without collective bargaining, employees (including faculty) have little true power in determining the terms and conditions of their employment; those terms are determined by the overall market for the type of labor involved, with some improvement possible depending on the benevolence of the governing board. Collective bargaining consolidates the minimal bargaining power possessed by each employee into the larger bargaining unit. While there is never a complete balancing of the scales, the relative power of labor and management is much more equal than would be the case in the absence of collective bargaining.

Most state laws contain further provisions to preclude stonewalling by management, requiring that each side negotiate in a good faith attempt to reach agreement. Enforcement mechanisms usually administered by a state agency are included if one side believes the other is not negotiating in good faith. When negotiations reach a serious stalemate, impasse procedures often call for the appointment of a neutral mediator or fact finder who will push the parties toward agreement. Consequently, there is always pressure on the governing board to reach an agreement with its employee unions.

The negotiations between the union and the college normally result in a written collective bargaining contract setting forth the various terms and conditions that have been agreed upon. Once the contract has been entered into, the college may not change any term or condition contained therein without going through a bargaining process that is generally prescribed in some detail by state law. In addition to matters covered in the contract, the college may not change matters within the scope of bargaining that have by a longstanding and uniform application become a standard past practice of the college. For example, if a college had an informal but consistent and longstanding practice of limiting all lecture classes to thirty-five students, the college may be required to notify and bargain with the faculty union before changing that limit. Obviously, one of the challenges of collective bargaining is determining whether a particular practice of the college has been sufficiently consistent and longstanding that the college is required to bargain with the union before changing the practice.

When a collective bargaining contract is agreed upon, it is generally enforced through a grievance process. If the exclusive representative believes that the college has violated a provision of the agreement, it files a grievance, initiating a process that usually leads to binding arbitration. A neutral arbitrator will issue a decision determining whether the contract has been violated and, if so, specifying a remedy.

The Impact of Collective Bargaining on Governance

The presence of collective bargaining and the collective bargaining contract itself significantly circumscribe management's traditional discretion in decision making. Obviously, the need to reach agreement with the union will slow board and management decision making on matters within the scope of bargaining. For example, salary increases may be stalled for an extended period of time—even into the ensuing academic year—if the union refuses to agree to the amount offered. When negotiations do not go smoothly, an inordinate amount of management time is consumed in bargaining sessions, board strategy discussions, and other activities necessary to reach resolution. Faculty morale during protracted stalemates usually declines, and the union often paints the board and management as unconcerned about, or even hostile to, the faculty. This perception affects the efficiency of day-to-day operations, as administration and faculty develop a negative attitude toward each other.

Collective bargaining may also have direct and indirect effects on shared governance entities and procedures, primarily on academic senate functions. In a nonunion environment, academic senates often are the major proponents of faculty concerns such as academic freedom. Many unions view the level of academic freedom on campus as a type of working condition that should be thoroughly addressed in the collective bargaining agreement. Some academic senate leadership may not want to give up authority in areas where it has traditionally exercised power and may resist shifting such matters to the collective bargaining process. Conflict often arises between the union and the senate, resulting in a relatively unsteady and sometimes inconsistent faculty voice in governance. At times the college management may become involved in refereeing the division of authority to deal with certain subjects between the senate and the faculty union. At best, a faculty union tends to limit academic senate activity to those matters—curriculum and instructional practices—that are clearly outside the scope of bargaining.

A second major effect of collective bargaining is management's need to employ a high degree of caution in taking almost any action, in order to preclude or reduce the possibility that an unfair labor practice or grievance may be filed against the college. When management takes action on any matter that falls within the mandatory scope of bargaining without first either obtaining the union's consent or bargaining the matter to impasse, an unfair practice charge can be filed against the college. Action that is in any way inconsistent with any provision of the collective bargaining agreement will result in a grievance. Management must carefully assess whether any action it is contemplating falls within either category. If so, the union must be brought into the picture. This extra step obviously slows implementation of new initiatives. It also tends to discourage innovations, since the immediate implementation of new ideas is often precluded.

NEW DIRECTIONS FOR COMMUNITY COLLEGES • DOI: 10.1002/cc

The presence of collective bargaining can also sharply reduce institutional flexibility. In the absence of collective bargaining, special individual arrangements regarding such matters as teaching hours and workload are sometimes worked out between college management and individual faculty members when special circumstances call for unique arrangements in the college's or faculty members' best interests. Such direct dealing is normally not allowed once an exclusive representative has been chosen, thereby requiring the college to go through the union to work out such special arrangements. This process is more time-consuming, and unions are reluctant to agree to such arrangements, insisting on strict uniformity of conditions for all faculty members.

The process for employee discipline is also severely impacted by the presence of a faculty union. Under the Weingarten doctrine, employees in a unit represented by a union have the right to have a representative of that union present at any meeting with a supervisory or management staff member that could lead to disciplinary action against the employee. This fact often leads to supervisors feeling intimidated about initiating disciplinary discussions; the specter of dealing with the shop steward (a more professional title is usually used by faculty unions) causes many supervisors to avoid predisciplinary discussions that are an important part of progressive discipline. Unions routinely attempt to hold management to perfect compliance with all evaluation and discipline procedures, which turns discipline measures into a major chore. This complication sometimes results in the college forgoing disciplinary action where such action is entirely appropriate.

A fourth significant impact of unionization is the introduction of a number of outsiders into the college's governance process (Rapp, 2007). Outside mediators and fact finders are brought in to attempt to move stalemated negotiations toward agreement. Arbitrators are delegated authority to resolve allegations of collective bargaining contract violation and render binding interpretations of contract language. The state's public employment relations board with jurisdiction over community colleges renders decisions on questions of which issues the college must negotiate, whether the college and union are negotiating in good faith, and whether the college has engaged in retaliation against employees for union activity. These outside individuals, who may have little background knowledge about the college and its functioning, make significant decisions on its governance. This aspect of unionization substantially diminishes the authority of the governing board.

Finally, the presence of a union that is an exclusive representative often results in an increased politicization of college governance. Unions, especially those affiliated with national organizations such as the American Federation of Teachers or National Education Association, frequently take an active role in both governing board elections and elections of state legislators who write the laws governing community colleges. Where an agency fee is imposed on unit members, the union may have a substantial income it can use not only to battle management but also to support candidates in board and statewide elections. The clout a union may have in a governing

NEW DIRECTIONS FOR COMMUNITY COLLEGES • DOI: 10.1002/cc

board election (where the voters generally may be relatively unknowledge-able about board candidates) can be substantial. This dynamic causes some board members concerned about reelection to be more accommodating to union concerns. In some cases the union manages to elect union-supported candidates as a majority of the board, creating difficulties for administra-tors trying to administer the college for the best interests of all constituen-cies—faculty, staff, students, and taxpayers—without being beholden to just one group.

It should be noted that certain broad areas of governance decisions are technically outside the scope of union concerns. Decisions such as whether to construct a new building or start a new instructional program are tradi-tionally management rights, and the union may not demand to bargain over them. However, since nearly all decisions of any significance have a finan-cial impact on the college, thus potentially affecting the funds available for faculty salaries and benefits, the union will often make vigorous attempts to influence those decisions. Depending on the strength of the particular fac-ulty union, it may play a major role in nearly all significant decisions ulti-mately made by the college's president and governing board.

Recommendations for Meeting the Challenges of a Union Environment

There is no question that managing a college in a union environment is more complex and challenging than managing in a nonunionized one. However, it is important for the administration in such a situation to accept the union as a fact of life. Negative comments about the union may be twisted and used against management in cases where the union alleges retaliation against its officers or in impasse proceedings. Any conduct indicating an anti-union bias may be thrown back at management in a variety of proceedings.

However, there are a number of precepts that, if followed, will make the challenges of the union environment less onerous. The following recom-mendations, based on the author's personal experience, are offered in an effort to make life easier for administrators faced with the difficulties of deal-ing with an exclusive representative.

Foster Good Relations. First and foremost, endeavor to develop a posi-tive working relationship with union leadership. The union-management relationship need not necessarily be completely adversarial. Management can facilitate a positive relationship by communicating as much as possible with union leadership so the union does not become aware of changes by receiving complaints from their members. A union leadership that is kept in the loop will feel much more collegial and invested in the success of the college. Sometimes union leadership attempts to obtain a concession from the college that is of extreme importance to its members but does not have a major impact on the operation of the college. Assisting the union leader-ship by responding to concerns that are clearly of great significance to union membership will enhance the membership's perception of union leadership as effective and should bring reciprocal cooperation from the leadership. Furthermore, it is not necessary for effective bargaining to use a fierce tone or to cling stubbornly to every aspect of every position. The style and tone of the negotiators at the bargaining table contribute heavily to the quality of the overall long-term relationship between the college and the union. A highly adversarial relationship will negatively impact the overall collegiality of the institution, impairing one of the most unique and valuable elements of the college workplace.

Be Familiar with Union Contracts and Policies. It is critically important that all management and supervisory employees become familiar with the collective bargaining contract and college policies and procedures. In addition, they should get in the habit of consulting the contract and college policies prior to taking action to ensure that the action will be completely consistent with the governing documents. If the union does not like the action taken, it will without fail scrutinize the contract and college policies looking for something that management may have overlooked. Unfortunately, in a union environment common sense is no longer the test for validity of administrative action, but rather the action's substantive compliance with policies, procedures, and the collective bargaining agreement. It is thus imperative to develop an effective training program to familiarize supervisors with the provisions of the contract and when they need to consult it. In addition, supervisors should be advised of the appropriate manager or office who will answer any questions they have about the interpretation of the contract or college policies and procedures.

Expect to Move Slowly. Unions tend to be process oriented; that is, they do not limit the ultimate authority of the college but rather impose many procedural steps before decisions can be implemented. Consequently, management must understand that it cannot move as rapidly as it may have done in other contexts. It will often be necessary to consult legal counsel on the interpretation of contract language or district policies to avoid the necessity of rescinding actions the college has taken without seeking legal advice.

Document All Conversations and Decisions. While it has become increasingly necessary for managers to document occurrences, communications, and decisions, it is even more important to do so in a union environment. Thorough notes should be taken of collective bargaining sessions, with all offers and responses documented in writing so that if an impasse is declared the college can show that it has bargained in good faith. In addition, such bargaining notes can be helpful in interpreting the contract language ultimately used in the collective bargaining agreement. Employee discipline in a union environment requires that both employee misconduct and warnings and reprimands to the employee be carefully documented in writing in order to build the kind of disciplinary case that will withstand the scrutiny of an outside arbitrator.

Educate the Board. It is also important to educate the college's governing board as to the myriad regulations and limitations of their authority when the faculty has chosen an exclusive representative. In particular, board members need to understand why action cannot be undertaken as rapidly as they desire. Most board members are unfamiliar with the complexities of collective bargaining and would benefit from training that illuminates the rights of the union and union members within the employer-employee relationship. In addition, the board should be thoroughly briefed on the issues being negotiated, so that board members will understand the arguments for both sides of the issues. Faculty unions will often contact individual board members concerning the matters being bargained, and members should be able to counter the arguments that may be made to them and explain the reasons for the board's position.

Employ Legal Counsel. In a union environment, it will be necessary to involve legal counsel much more extensively. It is difficult for a layperson, even an experienced college administrator, to wade through the many layers of collective bargaining law and procedures. Most union chapters have access to legal counsel who will carefully scrutinize the actions of the college administration, looking for flaws. Thus, it is imperative that proposed actions affecting the union or its membership be reviewed by the college's legal counsel. In addition, counsel should review the language of new collective bargaining provisions before they are signed off. This preventive step can save a great deal of time and expense later on, because any dispute arising from ambiguous language would have to be resolved through arbitration.

Do Not Be Intimidated. Extensive use of legal counsel will also assist administrators in following another significant precept: do not be intimidated by the union. Many administrators become distressed when they are contacted by the union about a decision they have made or by a problematic union employee. Administrators should remember that the union has a duty of fair representation (meaning that they must adequately investigate and present the employees' interests to management) and that contact by the union does not necessarily mean the union plans to undertake a full-scale attack on the administrator's actions. If the administrator has been consistent with college policy and the collective bargaining contract, there is little the union can do to challenge the administrative decision. It is also important that administrative personnel try not to take personally the union's questioning of their decisions. Such questioning is the union's role in the governance structure, and often the union is simply jumping through hoops to satisfy one or more of its membership. Anger or resentment at the union will not be helpful in explaining your position and convincing union leadership that the position is correct (Walker, 1981).

Remember That Contract Negotiations Are Not About Winning or Losing. Because the parties will have to continue to work together after negotiations for the year have concluded, a reasonable settlement that both parties can live with is a good one. A settlement that appears to management as a win but that angers the union (and especially the rank-and-file membership of the bargaining unit) may make employer-employee relations very difficult in the ensuing years.

NEW DIRECTIONS FOR COMMUNITY COLLEGES • DOI: 10.1002/cc

While there are many challenges arising from the presence of an exclusive representative organization on campus, it will be helpful in the long run to remember that there are also several advantages. It is much easier to communicate with a handful of union leaders than with the entire membership of the unit or even a variety of ad hoc committees. Good union leadership will carry forward explanations of administrative decisions that might otherwise cause great distress to the employees. For example, in difficult financial circumstances it often becomes necessary to lay off employees. Discussions with union leadership clearly outlining the financial picture and creating a comfort level that the appropriate employees have been selected for layoff may actually make such a difficult situation easier. The rank and file may be more secure in such a situation when they are convinced that their union leadership has carefully scrutinized the basis for the college's proposed action. In discipline situations, the union can be of similar assistance. Unions with good leadership will frequently advise problematic employees that they must shape up or move on to different jobs, because the college in fact does have sufficient cause to dismiss them and the union will not be able to save them. Again, when the employee hears it from the union rather than management, it is much more readily accepted. Finally, the grievance procedure usually provided by the contract provides a clearcut, readily available means for faculty to raise concerns that might otherwise fester or remain unknown to top management. And binding grievance arbitration provides a faster, more economical means of resolving employer-employee disputes than litigation through the courts.

Conclusion

Although the obvious complexities of a union environment create many challenges for a college administration, dealing with the union is a fact of life. More diligence and caution are required of management in such a situation, but an exclusive representative can nonetheless become part of a smoothly functioning governance system when the welfare of the institution takes precedence in all parties' decisions and activities.

References

Kaplin, W. A., and Lee, B. A. *The Law of Higher Education.* San Francisco: Jossey-Bass, 2006.
Rapp, J. A. *Education Law.* Newark, N.J.: LexisNexis, 2007.
Walker, D. E. *The Effective Administrator.* San Francisco: Jossey-Bass, 1981.
Wollett, D. "The Nature of Collective Bargaining and Its Relationship to Governance in Higher Education." In M. D. Abell (ed.), *Collective Bargaining in Higher Education: Its Implications for Governance and Faculty Status for Librarians.* Chicago: American Library Association, 1976.

TIMOTHY K. GARFIELD *is a partner in the San Diego law firm of Worley, Schwartz, Garfield, and Prairie, specializing in education law.*

This chapter describes the various approaches to internal shared governance utilized by community colleges, ranging from approaches that intentionally involve different constituents to those evolved from habit, tradition, and precedence.

Internal Governance in the Community College: Models and Quilts

Michael T. Miller, Jennifer M. Miles

Community college management has typically been cast as bureaucratic, allowing functional responsibilities of various offices to respond directly to specific needs and to respond directly to specified supervisors. One of the most popular and well-received depictions of this casting was offered by Birnbaum (1991), who aligned the clarity of community college mission with clean lines of authority.

The intention of the Birnbaum description was to demonstrate that the evolution of the contemporary community college was based largely on the ability of these colleges to demonstrate and live a mission and philosophy grounded in clearly articulated ideas and activities. Community colleges were designed as teaching institutions that provided relevant curriculum to their local communities. However, much within the higher education landscape has changed both in philosophy and operation, especially in the dynamic arena of community college education. Changes include an increased reliance on state instead of local revenue, reliance on and attention to philanthropic support, a growing role in transfer education, service to international populations, a third or fourth generation of faculty who use a great deal of intentionality in selecting their occupations, and a commitment to facility sophistication that includes a broader variety of services, types of facilities, and technology. The result is a changing and challenging approach to leadership and decision making.

WILEY
InterScience®
DISCOVER SOMETHING GREAT

NEW DIRECTIONS FOR COMMUNITY COLLEGES, no. 141, Spring 2008 © 2008 Wiley Periodicals, Inc.
Published online in Wiley InterScience (www.interscience.wiley.com) • DOI: 10.1002/cc.313

As community colleges have changed, their approach to internal decision making has both evolved and been the result of intentional activities and efforts to collaborate in the decision-making process. Although state and federal laws are specific about granting authority within higher education (Miles, A., 1997), community colleges have also recognized the need for collaborative governance as spelled out by the American Association of University Professors (1966). This chapter arises from the need to better understand the internal mechanisms that community colleges are using to facilitate the governance process within their institutions.

To best understand the governance practices in community colleges, the discussion should highlight faculty, student, staff, and trustee governance. For the purpose of this discussion, governance should be considered a process of decision making within the college, rather than an end unto itself. Consequently, governance broadly encompasses the strategies, practices, and habits of administrators as they discharge their administrative authority. This authority is typically granted through a state charter, either to an individual campus or to a collegewide system, and is legally held by the college's trustees. As Albert Miles (1997) noted and Pope updated (2003), the legal authority and ultimate responsibility for decision making within a college is held by and is the responsibility of the appointed administrators of an institution. However, as Evans (1999) argued, the discharge of this authority is enhanced and often improved when the process is focused on consensus building and garnering the input of those who will be most directly affected by the decision. In community colleges this means that governance is shared because it improves the institution, as opposed to governance mandated or dictated by a state agency or board of trustees.

Faculty Governance

The traditional depiction of the college faculty member was described by Adams (1988) as adversarial with administrators, a viewpoint often referenced in the literature on shared governance (Pope, 2004) and noted as a problem in effectively sharing governance (Miller, 2003). Yet within community colleges the issue of faculty responsibility in decision making has been seen as less problematic than in four-year institutions (Armstrong, 1999). The contemporary faculty member in community colleges has viewed this sharing of authority as not only an expectation, but something to be enjoyed and desired (Benton, 1997). Yet the notion of shared governance with faculty members in two-year colleges is relatively new and is seen with both optimism and caution.

As community colleges have evolved, they have adopted faculty members with expectations for involvement in governance. The forums developed to share authority span a spectrum of informal processes of consultation to elaborate senates and councils that elect representation. A dean of academic affairs at a community college in Mississippi reported that their faculty senate was active in reviewing institutional policy, but also lamented that the work of the senate was sporadic and inconsistent: its quality hinged on the abilities of the individuals elected to leadership positions. Armstrong's (1999) dissertation research profiling the activities of faculty senate over a decade illustrates this point. The issues addressed by the faculty senate he studied ranged from tobacco use policies to office space assignments to merit pay, campus appearance, and student record management. He concluded that faculty senates do indeed provide a sounding board for administration, but they also spend considerable time discussing and considering topics outside their purview. Pope (2003) reinforced this finding in reviewing literature about faculty senates in two-year colleges. He concluded that they do allow for input, but their impact is questionable.

Some of the behaviors of community college faculty senates may be related to the generational shift occurring in two-year colleges. Williams, Gore, Broches, and Lostoski (1987) indicated that faculty involvement in governance was correlated strongly with issue relevance and the personal motivation of the faculty member (suggesting, for example, age and career stage as variables). However, Eaton (1991), Laabs (1987), and Hawthorne (1991) suggest that the changing composition of community college faculty may affect both expectations and outcomes related to sharing authority. These authors argue that as more community college faculty members have begun to pursue this career path intentionally (not resorting to the community college faculty as an afterthought or an alternative to secondary school faculty), they have also come to embrace a culture or expectation of inclusive decision making. This trend represents a change from Pope's (2003) observation that the initial generation of community college faculty members were recruited from secondary schools, where they rarely expected to participate in governance.

Faculty in community colleges play an instrumental role in determining program curriculum, typically with insight and advice from professionals working in various disciplines and colleges that accept their transfer students. This curriculum development often has direct consequences on enrollment and completion, particularly when students enroll in specific occupationally related disciplines because of their desire to work in a specific field. Examples include faculty in traditional vocational areas who collaborate with local business and industry to refine course requirements and faculty who teach transfer curricula and consult with four-year university faculty on curriculum issues. Rural community colleges in particular make special efforts to align curriculum with job entry requirements and a student population that wishes to remain in the local area (Katsinas and Miller, 1998).

Many community colleges also employ a substantial number of part-time faculty members, and these individuals are only marginally involved in localized decision making. As full-time employees in other fields, they may consult on curriculum and make recommendations for additions or deletions as relevant to their field.

NEW DIRECTIONS FOR COMMUNITY COLLEGES • DOI: 10.1002/cc

In general terms, faculty members play an important role in consulting on the direction of a college—both through formalized conduits such as senates, councils, or associations and through less formal pressures such as individual meetings with administrators. As administrators play an increasingly external role in fundraising and dealing with the business community (Pope, 2004), this consultative activity grows in importance and can become a framework for decision making in academic affairs and a broad array of college affairs.

Student Governance

Student involvement in higher education governance has been problematic since the founding of the earliest colleges in North America (Miles, J., 1997). Students want conveniences on the one hand, yet also demand the rigor necessary for their life beyond college. This is particularly true in community colleges, where many students expect occupational training or affordable transfer education while simultaneously expecting a high level of service in certain types of atmospheres, such as new and technologically enhanced facilities. As the student body in community colleges changes to include more traditional-age students and more women (Safarik, Wolgemuth, and Kees, 2003), the involvement of students in institutional decision making has also changed to reflect the demands of full-time students with a different set of expectations about institutional services, roles, and offerings.

Student involvement in governance often mirrors faculty involvement efforts, including elected representatives from various disciplines or academic units. However, with the broad spectrum of students represented in community colleges, such representation is difficult. With substantial numbers of part-time students in vastly diverse programs, the contemporary community college serves a wide spectrum of students, including those enrolling to complete a course for a bachelor's degree at another institution, those seeking retraining for the workplace, those pursuing remedial or literacy education, and those hoping to complete a general education curriculum that will take them closer to a four-year degree. With the growing number of traditional students on community college campuses, this disparity is more sharply articulated by the demands of traditional students expecting opportunities to prove themselves and get involved in what they consider to be traditional college opportunities, including social networking opportunities and out-of-class organizations that augment their academic experience.

Indeed, student involvement in governance can be an important element in the life of an institution. In addition to teaching students principles of democracy, representation, and responsibility, involvement gives administrators and faculty opportunities to consider different points of view and allows decisions to be made at the most local level. Involvement in activities such as representative governance can also play an important role in the personal and social development of the college student (Kuh and Lund, 1994).

However, as mentioned earlier, student involvement in governance can be problematic. In addition to issues of student maturity and willingness to take responsibility for immediate and long-term behaviors, student government has been subject to extreme peer pressure and special interest group dominance (Randall, Miller, and Nadler, 1999). In addition, the qualifications of students can become an issue for administrators when those students willing to be involved may not be the best prepared to deal with the issues put before them. A faculty member at a community college in central Alabama who was interviewed for this chapter commented: "We have a student advisory group that meets with the president, but they don't have any real power. I don't think they would know what to do with it." Conversely, a dean of students at a community college in Kansas commented: "We make use of an elected student senate, and they meet with the president and me a couple of times a semester. While they don't have any official power, it helps us make better decisions about a lot of things."

When sharing governance community colleges must also struggle with the concept of *in loco parentis,* meaning the role the college takes in place of students' parents (Ghosh, Whipple, and Bryan, 2001; Miles, 1997; Hodgkinson, 1971). Although most community college students commute to their campuses, the college must consider its legal and developmental role in empowering students to make decisions and the students' involvement in institutional operations. Therein lies the particular issue for community college leaders looking to empower students and to use shared governance as an educational tool for student development. Little research articulates what is happening on community college campuses in this regard, but even a cursory review of web sites or personal interviews with community college leaders demonstrates an array of approaches ranging from elected senates that disburse student fee money to presidential meetings with random students to talk about the affairs of the institution.

This eclectic approach to shared governance with students is seen in most types of higher education institutions (Miles, Miller, and Nadler, forthcoming) and is commonly relegated to procedural input rather than substantive input (Miles, J., 1997). Community colleges thus recognize the need to hear students' voices when making decisions; however, there is little vestment of real power with student groups.

Staff Governance

The largest component of any higher education institution's budget is personnel, and community colleges are no exception. Although the largest segment of an institution's budget is typically devoted to instructional salaries, the investment in staff and administrative positions has grown substantially during the past two decades (Rhodes, 2001). Staff positions have arisen in areas such as governmental relations, technology support, and fundraising, and the bureaucratic illustration of community colleges by Birnbaum (1991) has been reinforced. In a bureaucracy, positions are allocated specific authority, reporting channels, and a span of control to execute their responsibilities. When these individuals are involved in shared governance and internal decision making, however, these lines can become blurred and create both opportunities and challenges for the institution.

The benefits of sharing authority with staff include the traditional human resource management findings identified by Evans (1999): a greater acceptance of decisions, a more central approach to decision making that includes input from individuals closest to the problem, cross-functioning teams that can support each other, an increased feeling of value by the staff members, and a greater number of responses potentially developed to resolve problems or challenges. Conversely, by attempting to share authority with individuals who are specifically charged in other areas, the college may see a disproportionate shift of authority to those who are not compensated to make decisions in a specific area, a greater time commitment to bring individuals together to meet and make decisions, and a question of competence and confidence to make decisions that affect others.

No baseline data were available to illustrate how community colleges are using staff senates. Subsequently, five college presidents were interviewed to form an initial impression of their use and reliance. A president from a California community college commented: "With such strong unions, we don't do much. We have a back-to-school and holiday party, and a staff appreciation picnic in the spring, but that's about it." In Nebraska, Kansas, and Illinois, presidents portrayed a very different approach. From Illinois, a president reported: "We have an elected staff council, and I meet with them once or twice a semester. Their input is usually pretty good, but it's mostly advice and they only make recommendations to me." The president from Kansas responded: "Our staff council is real and makes real decisions. They have a small budget for professional development, bring in speakers and buy books or videos, and at times deal with issues of merit pay and salary equity."

While this area certainly warrants further study, the literature and profiling interviews point to an inconsistent use of staff in governance. Although almost every community college makes use of cross-functional committees for certain topical areas, there is little evidence to suggest that these approaches are evenly distributed across the community college landscape. Nonetheless, presidents and other community college leaders can potentially find staff involvement in governance a critical tool for realigning an institution's mission or making institution-changing decisions.

Trustees' Role

All fifty states currently have some form of state oversight for higher education, typically referred to as a board of trustees, governors, or overseers (Davis, 2002). In addition, most states with comprehensive systems of community colleges rely on locally elected boards of trustees, typically representing the geographic area of service for the college. These community-based boards can provide immediate input and response to any number of college issues, regardless of whether the campus's administration welcomes input. Perhaps the greatest benefit of local board input lies in its ability to provide feedback and informal assessment of the quality of the college's offerings and programs. Board members can together form an apt barometer of the college's impact and are uniquely situated to assess the quality of graduates. They can provide this perspective through personal relationships with the local consumers of college services and through personal interaction with neighbors, church members, social club associates, and others.

Unfortunately, in community colleges with local board control this feedback is often isolated, politically motivated, and not representative of the overall impact or quality of the college. With local access and oversight of the college, board members may be inclined to offer unwarranted input or make unreasonable demands based on personal agendas. Like school superintendents in K–12 districts, college leaders may end up devoting a significant portion of their time to board relations. In addition, the demands of the local governing board can affect curriculum relevance and content, facility appearance, adjunct faculty use, and even student admission.

Most community college administrators under local board control meet with board members on a monthly or quarterly basis to discuss a predetermined agenda, and deal with personnel matters in executive sessions whenever possible. College leaders also find the use of advisory boards important tools for dissipating the political demands placed upon them. By using advisory boards and committees for academic and occupational programs, college leaders are more appropriately situated to keep academic and curricular issues in the internal decision-making realm of college affairs.

Other Influences on Governance

In addition to faculty, student, staff, and trustee governance issues, college leaders must deal with a host of pressures that can affect internal decision making and the processes for making those decisions. These pressures include external accrediting bodies that may have specific protocols for meeting curriculum and admission standards; unions for faculty and staff where individuals meet formally with college administrators to deal with such issues as merit pay, compensation, and workload; and special interest groups within the college. Special interest groups can exert an especially high level of power and influence in decision making, depending on the issue and its relevance to the group (Williams, Gore, Broches, and Lostoski, 1987). Examples of such influence include the collective actions of multiethnic, female, or part-time faculty who gather informally or formally to bring about change or resolution to a specific issue.

Conclusion

There is no single model or classification of structures that can enhance or dictate the decision-making process at all community colleges. Instead, institutions use a wide variety of strategies, emphasizing different elements or pieces of the process at different times and in response to the needs of different issues. The result is a more quiltlike approach to decision making, where administrators can call upon different groups as needed to cover different issues and problems.

Following are specific advantages arising from this quiltlike approach to decision making.

Good practices. Research and practice consistently demonstrate that open communication and consensus building among all employees lead to higher morale, motivation, retention, and organizational effectiveness (Evans, 1999). In practice this means college administrators will have greater success adapting their colleges to societal changes by involving multiple constituencies in the decision-making process.

Effectiveness and efficiency. College leaders need to place internal governance procedures within the broader constraints of the college's operations. Effective presidents use a special skill to determine when shared governance is appropriate and when and where to involve multiple constituents. Not all issues need immediate action, and some will benefit from a dialogue that includes multiple perspectives. Conversely, some issues do need immediate action and cannot afford the luxury of campuswide discussion. The key to success, then, is to build protocols and procedures, or models, for the resolution of different types of decisions and issues, and to stay the course, even through difficult times.

Clarity of roles. College administrators are legally bound to share authority with trustees, and most internal governance activities are consultative. College leaders need to specify these requirements and spend time educating those participating in governance about their expectations and roles. However, it is equally important for college leaders to demonstrate that they value input from constituent groups by spending time explaining processes, decisions, and why input was or was not accepted.

Change. As higher education as a whole strives to reflect more accurately the needs of its stakeholders, it is important for community colleges to remain responsive to their service areas. Thus college leaders need to involve each of the internal governing bodies in discussions of necessary

NEW DIRECTIONS FOR COMMUNITY COLLEGES • DOI: 10.1002/cc

changes and the potential impact of those changes on all college constituencies.

Internal governance in the community college continues to evolve to represent the viewpoints and ideas of a variety of internal and external stakeholders. As this chapter has shown, a variety of mechanisms is available to help college leaders and trustees hear the voices of those closest to students and services, but no single model will serve to hear and consider all these voices. What has evolved is a series of processes that provide access to decision making and to future research that can demonstrate best practices for implementing change. These mechanisms will become an excellent resource for the coming generation of community college faculty, staff, and administrators.

References

Adams, H. *The Academic Tribes.* (2nd ed.) Chicago: University of Illinois, 1988.

American Association of University Professors. *1966 Statement on Government of Colleges and Universities.* Washington, D.C.: American Association of University Professors, 1966.

Armstrong, W. P. "Trends and Issues of a Community College Faculty Senate: Jefferson State Community College, 1987–1997." Unpublished doctoral dissertation, University of Alabama, Tuscaloosa, 1999.

Benton, C. J. "Faculty Involvement in Two-Year College Governance." Unpublished doctoral dissertation, University of Alabama, Tuscaloosa, 1997.

Birnbaum, R. *How Colleges Work: The Cybernetics of Academic Organization and Leadership.* San Francisco: Jossey-Bass, 1991.

Davis, H. *A Political Model of Higher Education Governance and Policy Reform Adoption.* Houston: Institute for Higher Education Law and Governance, 2002.

Eaton, J. "The Coming Transformation of Community Colleges." *Planning for Higher Education,* 1991, 21(1), 1–7.

Evans, J. P. "Benefits and Barriers to Shared Authority." In M. Miller (ed.), *Responsive Academic Decision Making Involving Faculty in Higher Education Governance.* Stillwater, Okla.: New Forums, 1999.

Ghosh, A. K., Whipple, T. W., and Bryan, G. A. "Student Trust and Its Antecedents in Higher Education." *Journal of Higher Education,* 2001, 72(3), 322–340.

Hawthorne, E. M. "Anticipating a New Generation of Community College Faculty Members." *Journal of College Science Teachers,* May 1991, pp. 365–368.

Hodgkinson, H. L. *College Governance: The Amazing Thing Is That It Works at All.* Washington, D.C.: ERIC Clearinghouse on Higher Education and the George Washington University, 1971.

Katsinas, S. G., and Miller, M. T. "Vocational Education in Rural Community Colleges: Contemporary Issues and Problems." *Journal of Vocational Education Research,* 1998, 23(2), 159–169.

Kuh, G., and Lund, J. P. "What Students Gain from Participating in Student Government." In M. C. Terrell and M. J. Cuyjet (eds.), *Developing Student Government Leadership.* New Directions for Student Services, no. 66. San Francisco: Jossey-Bass, 1994.

Laabs, T. R. "Community College Tenure: Teach or Research?" *Community/Junior College Quarterly,* 1987, 11, 267–273.

Miles, A. S. *College Law.* (2nd ed.) Tuscaloosa, Ala.: Sevgo, 1997.

Miles, J. M. "Student Leader Perceptions of Increasing Participation in Self-Governance." Unpublished doctoral dissertation, University of Alabama, Tuscaloosa, 1997.

Miles, J. M., Miller, M. T., and Nadler, D. P. "A National Study of Improving Participation in Student Self-Governance Leadership." *College Student Services Journal of Research and Practice,* forthcoming.

Miller, M. T. *Improving Faculty Governance.* Stillwater, Okla.: New Forums, 2003.

Pope, M. L. "Faculty Governance in Community Colleges: A Distinct Perspective on Broad-Based Decision Making." In M. Miller and J. Caplow (eds.), *Policy and University Faculty Governance.* Greenwich, Conn.: Information Age, 2003.

Pope, M. L. "A Conceptual Framework of Faculty Trust and Participation in Governance." In W. G. Tierney and V. M. Lechuga (eds.), *Restructuring Shared Governance in Higher Education.* New Directions for Higher Education, no. 127. San Francisco: Jossey-Bass, 2004.

Randall, K. P., Miller, M. T., and Nadler, D. P. "Reviving an SGA: A Case Study." *Journal of College Orientation and Transition,* 1999, 7(1), 33–35.

Rhodes, F.H.T. *The Creation of the Future: The Role of the American University.* Ithaca, N.Y.: Cornell University Press, 2001.

Safarik, L., Wolgemuth, J. R., and Kees, N. L. "A Feminist Critique About Women Published in the Community College Journal of Research and Practice: 1990–2000." *Community College Journal of Research and Practice,* 2003, 27, 769–786.

Williams, D., Gore, W., Broches, C., and Lostoski, C. "One Faculty's Perceptions of Its Governance Role." *Journal of Higher Education,* 1987, 58, 629–655.

MICHAEL T. MILLER *is professor of higher education and head of the Department of Rehabilitation, Human Resources, and Communication Disorders at the University of Arkansas.*

JENNIFER M. MILES *is assistant professor of higher education at the University of Arkansas.*

5

This chapter uses Kentucky and Iowa as case studies to identify the contextual factors affecting the relationship between workforce development and state community college governance.

The Effect of the Community College Workforce Development Mission on Governance

Janice Nahra Friedel

Community colleges were built on the foundations that emerged from the integration of junior colleges with postsecondary vocational institutions. As the 1980s approached and the majority of these institutions entered their third decade, the nation adjusted to the radical shift from a manufacturing-driven economy to a service- and information-driven economy. As state legislatures developed policy to create and retain employers, community colleges became the primary tool for economic and workforce development.

This chapter explores the relationship between the workforce development mission and community college governance. It begins with a brief overview of the evolution of the community college workforce development function and the increasing prominence of workforce development initiatives in public policy. The chapter then uses case studies from Kentucky and Iowa to demonstrate how states with similar economic and workforce development conditions stay focused on similar goals but end up on opposite ends of the continuum of state coordination, control, and governance. Thus, contextual understanding of the evolution of a system becomes a key to understanding governance and the workforce development mission.

New Directions for Community Colleges, no. 141, Spring 2008 © 2008 Wiley Periodicals, Inc.
Published online in Wiley InterScience (www.interscience.wiley.com) • DOI: 10.1002/cc.314

45

Increasing Expansion of the Workforce Development Functions

Occupational education became a major community college mission in the 1950s and 1960s as state governors, legislators, and college administrators pushed for expansion of the vocational function of community colleges as a means to stimulate state economies. Through their government-subsidized employee training, community colleges developed a distinct training niche and served as tools in attracting businesses and industries to their states and region (Brint and Karabel, 1989). In the early 1980s, the U.S. economy experienced a radical transformation driven by the displacement of large manufacturers to overseas production plants and the shift to a service-oriented and information-driven economy. The Midwest region experienced a major agricultural reces-sion fostered by changes in national farm policy and the rapid erosion of its manufacturing base. As state economies declined, community colleges moved to center stage in efforts to revive and stimulate the economic conditions of local communities, regions, and states. In attempts to curb outsourcing, states developed public policies, including subsidized training and tax incentives, to retain employers and to attract new businesses and investments.

Community colleges responded by rapidly expanding contract training and noncredit offerings and services. Community colleges saw contract training as a means to accrue enrollments and revenues and to develop political alliances (Dougherty and Bakia, 2000; Grubb, Bell, Bragg and Rus-sam, 1997). Much of this work was performed and coordinated through noncredit instructional units of the community colleges; these units were often separate from the traditional credit and occupational instructional units (Jacobs and Dougherty, 2006). Unimpeded by the structure of the credit functions and faculties, these customized contract units had great flexibility in curriculum design, faculty qualifications, and delivery method. These units became recognized for their ability to respond quickly to the needs of employers and businesses.

Economic development strategies were grounded in the premise that a well-trained workforce would attract and retain businesses and indus-tries in the state; thus evolved the hand-in-hand relationship between workforce and economic development. However, public policies varied greatly from state to state, hindered or fostered by the governance and con-text of the state systems of community colleges.

During the 1970s and 1990s, the United States federal government developed an array of job training programs to address occupational educa-tion, unemployment, and poverty issues. "Despite high hopes, these major initiatives are examples of the failure of broad-based, inefficient government policies" (McCabe and Pincus, 1997, p. 3). Comprehensive Employment and Training Administration (CETA) was signed into law by President Nixon in 1973 and had lackluster results; its major pitfall was that government jobs were given to the chronically unemployed, never providing them with tangible skills needed for employment in the private sector (McCabe and Pincus, 1997). Its legislative successor, the Job Training Partnership Act (JTPA) of 1982, was the Reagan administration's answer to joblessness. JTPA allocated funds for remedial training, classroom vocational technical training, and on-the-job training, but provided no funds for public service employment, work experience allowances, wages, or other type of income maintenance (McCabe and Pincus, 1997). These programs were aimed at the most marginalized citizens and gave the states a clear mandate to use the federal resources in consultation with private industry to establish programs. Most recently the passage of the Workforce Investment Act in 2000 mandated the coordination of workforce funding and efforts.

Broadly speaking, workforce development programs have been implemented to address two significant labor issues. Federal programs coordinated through the United States Department of Labor have historically targeted chronically unemployed and displaced workers. The workforce development one-stop centers offer assessment, career counseling, limited training, and job placement of clients. In contrast, the United States Department of Education has focused on the broad base of the employment spectrum: the education and training of new entrants into the workforce and incumbent worker education. These components include vocational and technical education, adult basic education, English for second language learners, and high school completion and GED.

Community colleges have been designated the lead agency to provide workforce training in at least nineteen states, and in most others they are prominent players in the workforce development system. "Where they are effective, community college workforce development programs further both the career goals of workers and the business objectives of employers. To the extent that they help local residents secure well-paying jobs and advance in their careers, and also assist employers to hire, retain, and enhance the performance of their employees, community colleges have become a force in the economic development of their communities" (Education Commission of the States, 2002, p. 2). It is important to note that the activities of workforce development and economic development often overlap in their purposes at the community college (Grubb, Bell, Bragg, and Russam, 1997). In addition, community colleges are committed to preparing a workforce with both the academic and technical skills needed to successfully compete in the world market. They strengthen the economic base and reskill the workforce by helping adults prepare for the world of work or upgrade their work skills by providing opportunity for the development of higher levels of literacy, basic academic skills, and occupational and technical skills.

As the landscapes of local, regional, and state economies have changed and the community colleges have responded to workforce development needs, their offerings and enrollments in contracted classes and noncredit

48   GOVERNANCE IN THE COMMUNITY COLLEGE

courses have altered the nature of their mission. Flexibility, responsiveness, and meeting lifelong learning needs are hallmarks of their missions. But the expectations are high; community colleges are often designated as a primary driver of a state's economic development through the workforce preparation and development function. Such pressure has in many cases resulted in the state's examination and redesign of the community college governance structure.

The Changing Landscape of Community College Governance and State Coordination

Community college governance and state coordination vary from state to state and have changed over the years. Between 1997 and 2002, eight states enacted significant changes in their state-level postsecondary education structure, with significant change defined as eliminating, establishing, or changing the authority of state-level boards. These states were Arkansas, Colorado, Florida, Kansas, Kentucky, Louisiana, Utah, and West Virginia. During this same period, Hawaii, Maine, Maryland, North Dakota, and Texas made important changes in governance or the role of state-level boards of systems. The major categories of change in state structure and governance from 1997 to 2002 include comprehensive reforms linked to a public agenda for the future of the state, establishment of K–16 and K–20 structures, state structures for community and technical colleges, and decentralization and deregulation (McGuinness, 2002).

The Kentucky Experience

Kentucky's lackluster educational and economic performance during much of the twentieth century propelled its legislature to an educational and workforce development reform agenda during the 1980s and 1990s. The state's budget was cut twelve times between 1981 and 1994—more than any other state in the nation. The workforce's relative lack of education was less of an issue when "agriculture, mining, distilling, and textile production were the state's economic mainstays, but it became a major competitive disadvantage with the growth of the knowledge-based economy" (National Governors Association, 2001). Things began to change in 1986, when Toyota located its major North American automotive plant in Richmond, Kentucky, just north of Lexington. "By the mid 1990s, Kentucky policymakers and business leaders were keen to repeat the Toyota experience. They recognized that to attract and retain world class firms, more Kentuckians would need more and better education" (National Governors Association, 2001, p. 3). An influential and powerful force advocating change came from JobQuEST, a coalition of business and education organizations that pushed for education reform at all levels, including postsecondary and higher education. This appeal for change from the busi-

NEW DIRECTIONS FOR COMMUNITY COLLEGES • DOI: 10.1002/cc

ness sector and then the governor became the impetus for a legislative agenda to restructure the governance of Kentucky's community college system.

The hallmark of Paul Patton's tenure as governor of the state of Kentucky may be his political decision to take on, and success in tackling, the political goliath of the University of Kentucky (UK) and its formidable leader, Charles E. Wethington. The state's flagship university had built a loyal constituency of political strength buttressed with alumni dispersed throughout the state and a system of fourteen community colleges geographically dispersed and strategically located. The system of community colleges was an essential part of the university's strategy to accomplish the extension mission of the land-grant university. The UK board of trustees was the governing board of the UK community college system, and each community college had an advisory board with a very limited role. A system of technical colleges under the auspices of the Workforce Cabinet also had institutions dispersed across the state. In addition, the eight regional universities offered associate degree and other two-year programs unique to their geographic area and programs. Lack of coordination between the various sectors of postsecondary education, as well as barriers to students' transition across institutions and programs, contributed to the governance initiative. Recognition of the changing landscape of the economy, increasing global competitiveness, the increasingly technical nature of work, and a desire to leverage limited state resources in a coordinated workforce development strategy fueled the public discourse and legislative initiative.

The workforce development function was dispersed principally across the technical and community college state systems. Technical degrees granted by the technical colleges were terminal and did not articulate to the UK Community College System and baccalaureate degree-granting institutions.

Features of the UK Community College System included systemwide standardization of the curriculum, enabling colleges across the state to adopt already developed and approved curriculum. Students could easily transfer from one community college to another, as well as to the UK. Faculties were tenured across the system. At the same time, the process for program development and approval was protracted, requiring approval from a system committee of faculty representatives from all community colleges. An institution's ability to respond to local needs could be hindered by faculty from other colleges. Budgets were line-item approved at the system level. New faculty positions were approved and budgeted at the system level. Contract and customized training was in its infancy and completely self-supporting. There was no institutional support to initiate the important contracted or customized training function of the college, and connectiveness between the credit and noncredit functions of the college was hindered by the ingrained nature of the tenure system. Although individual presidents had made overtures to the Kentucky Technical College in their region, the leadership of the UK Community College System declined suggestions from the presidents to collaborate with the system on workforce development initiatives and programs.

The legislature of the state of Kentucky completely revamped higher education with passage of the Post-Secondary Improvement Act. The bill called for the University of Kentucky to become a top public research university by 2020, the University of Louisville to become a predominant metro research university, programs of distinction and access to the baccalaureate degree to be expanded through the eight regional universities, and the establishment of a new entity—the Kentucky Community and Technical College System (KCTCS). The primary vehicle for accomplishing the legislation's goal of offering access to two-year liberal arts and technical degrees, remedial instruction, workforce training, and continuing education would be through the merger of the technical college system operated by the Workforce Development Cabinet with the community colleges of the UK. A new governance structure was established: the Kentucky Community and Technical College Board.

KCTCS has evolved into a system of comprehensive community colleges recognized as the primary workforce development vehicle for the commonwealth. In fall 2005, 84,931 students enrolled in more than six hundred KCTCS credit program options. Through sixteen colleges located at sixty-five campuses, KCTCS is the largest provider of postsecondary education and workforce training in the state. Its programs range from the Kentucky Employability Skills Certificates and general educational development testing to associate degree programs and incumbent worker–contracted training.

Kentucky and Iowa are two states at opposite ends of the spectrum of statewide coordination and governance. As summarized earlier, the highly centralized UK Community College System was merged with the Kentucky Technical College System to become the Kentucky Community and Technical College System (KCTCS), an equally centralized state system, but with a clear focus on the workforce development mission. The context, evolution, faculties, institutional culture, and governance of the UK system was not perceived as customer-focused, responsive, flexible or regionally driven. The context that gave rise to the new KCTCS was vastly different from the context of the governance debate in Iowa.

The Iowa Experience

The context and evolution of the Iowa community colleges is embedded in the state's commitment to local autonomy and control for both K–12 school districts and public community colleges. Iowa's system was largely shaped by the legislation passed in 1965, which was fueled by the increased demand for education and training for veterans and baby boomers reaching college age. Community colleges were formed through the merger of local school district–based junior colleges and postsecondary vocational schools, and have evolved into the colleges of first choice of the majority of Iowans entering higher education (Varner, 2006). From the very beginning, the Iowa experience has highlighted comprehensiveness and nonduplication across the public postsecondary sector.

Vocational education, college transfer or prebaccalaureate degree programs, and programs for post–high school age students to complete their high school education and obtain vocational and job training opportunities were included in Iowa's community college enabling legislation. In the 1980s, the community colleges responded to the increasing needs of nontraditional students and displaced homemakers by expanding their noncredit, continuing education, and contracted training functions.

In 1983, the Iowa legislature made substantial efforts to stimulate economic development and in the process advanced community colleges toward their goal of workforce development. The Iowa Industrial New Jobs Training Act was established to provide support for the customized training of new employees of new business start-ups and to expand basic sector businesses. No up-front funding was required; the colleges issued tax-exempt or taxable bonds for up to ten years on behalf of the eligible businesses. Proceeds from the bond sales were used to finance the training and related administrative costs. The principal and interest payments on the bonds were paid using a diversion of state income tax withholding from the new employees. Instead of sending these employees' withholding to the state's general fund, employers diverted the funds to the community colleges. When the bonds were retired, the state withholding was released to the general fund. The program was a powerful incentive because employers received customized training for their workers at little or no cost and funding was drawn from the taxes of new employees. This program was coordinated on a statewide basis through the Iowa Department of Economic Development.

The mission of Iowa's community colleges was profoundly affected by the 1983 enactment of the Iowa Industrial New Jobs Training Act, now referred to simply as 260E legislation. The legislation drew the Iowa community colleges into customized contracted training much earlier than community colleges in other states (Varner, 2006). The 260E program added the fourth pillar to the foundational programs of arts and sciences, career education, and adult and continuing education already offered by the community colleges. 260E was a watershed event: "It helped individual colleges to establish strong working relationships and credibility with the businesses within their regions and develop a politically powerful constituency. From 1983–2005, Iowa's community colleges issued more than $466 million in bonds, through 1,800 training agreements, helping to support the pledged creation of more than 126,000 relatively well-paying jobs" (Varner, 2006, p. 57).

The Iowa legislature realized that the growth of the state's economy could not rely solely on the attraction of new businesses and industries to the state. Action was needed to retain the existing employer base. In 1985, the Iowa Jobs Training Act (later called Iowa Code Chapter 260F) was passed to provide customized job training services to the incumbent workers of eligible businesses. Participating businesses received loans delivered through the community colleges that were forgiven if they completed the training program within the agreed-upon time frame and retrained a sufficient number of employees. Community colleges sponsored the businesses, delivered their training, and coordinated the program with the Iowa Department of Economic Development. The assistance available ranged from basic skills to highly specialized training for new positions. Companies eligible included those engaged in manufacturing, processing, assembly of products, warehousing, wholesaling, research and development, and the provision of services to out-of-state customers. Qualifying businesses could group into consortia for training assistance. In 1995 a permanent and predictable funding source was secured for the Iowa Jobs Training Program through the establishment of the Workforce Development Fund. By the end of 2005, more than 89,000 workers in 650 companies participated in more than a thousand projects through the 260F projects.

Iowa's community colleges have their roots in the public K–12 school structure through the merger of the K–12 district–affiliated junior colleges and postsecondary vocational schools and technical colleges. Each community college has a locally elected board of directors with primary governance responsibilities; the State Board of Education has K–14 responsibilities, including statewide coordination and state oversight responsibilities of the community colleges. These governance characteristics and the maturity of the community colleges position them for strong roles in regional development and high school or redesign efforts; community colleges play an important role in providing high school student access to both quality career and technical programs and arts and sciences courses. In 2006, 25,578 high school students were enrolled in community college credit courses, of which 5,328 earned college credit in career and technical programs. High school students comprised approximately 21 percent of the total credit community college enrollment that year.

Since 1997, the enrollment at Iowa's community colleges has consistently demonstrated high penetration into the adult population. About one of every four Iowans between the ages of eighteen and sixty-four enrolls in a community college course annually (both credit and noncredit). The importance of the noncredit, customized training offerings of the colleges is evident in the fiscal year 2006 enrollment of 287,073, as compared to the credit enrollment of 121,753.

Studies of the governance structure of Iowa community colleges were legislatively mandated in 1987, and again in 1999. The first study resulted in recommendations to strengthen the Iowa State Board of Education and the Iowa Department of Education's oversight by creating the Community College Council of the Iowa State Board of Education and the Division of Community Colleges and Workforce Development within the Iowa Department of Education. The purposes of the 1999 study were to identify options for restructuring the community college governance system, examine the need for greater uniformity and how to best plan for the future, and how to most efficiently leverage colleges' resources.

Unlike the case in Kentucky, there was no public or nonpartisan call or proposal for change in governance in Iowa; there was no alliance or consolidation of business around a governance debate. During the Iowa study, considerable discussion centered on local governance boards and increased accountability and coordination at the state level. Although local governance can impede systemwide coordination and planning, there was strong support for local control in Iowa generally and in community college circles specifically. It was legislatively mandated that the Community College Council develop a five-year statewide strategic plan for the community colleges and that the Iowa Department of Education develop a statewide community college management information system. Local governance was preserved, and the Iowa State Board of Education retained its K–14 responsibilities.

Future Considerations

It is interesting to note that in both Kentucky and Iowa community colleges are identified as the primary workforce development agencies and drivers of economic development. However, the governance study outcomes were quite different. In Kentucky, major political constituents had perceived the governance and administrative structures as a hindrance to a workforce development agenda; in Iowa, the community colleges were already successfully functioning in a workforce development leadership role. Nonetheless, institutions cannot rest on their laurels.

Workforce development is now a national priority. Thomas Friedman's (2005) *The World Is Flat* has catapulted the workforce development issue to national prominence. The dual systems of the Kentucky technical colleges under the Kentucky Workforce Board and the University of Kentucky Community College System under the governance of the University of Kentucky Board of Trustees were perceived as duplicative and often conflictual. In Kentucky the goal of the governance initiative was to create a unified, unduplicative system that combined the training and retraining expertise of the workforce board with the collegiate transfer function of the community colleges. The result was a new system of comprehensive community colleges under one governance structure, accompanied by a substantial infusion of state funds to support the workforce mission of the newly formed Kentucky Community and Technical College System (KCTCS). The Iowa community college study recommended the development of a statewide community college strategic plan and the monitoring and accountability of the community colleges toward the accomplishment of a set of priorities agreed on in the planning process. The Iowa Department of Education was charged with the development of a management information system to enable the state to report statewide data about the system, local governance was reaffirmed, and no additional funds were allocated in support of these statewide initiatives. In Iowa, the importance of the capacity to report on the system of community colleges became paramount.

Even in a state like Iowa with a long and successful history of community college leadership in workforce development, community colleges must be diligent and resourceful in telling their story through quantitative and anecdotal data. The dispersion of education, workforce, and economic development functions across three state agencies may result in the perception of a disparate and duplicative system. The results of all community college activity must be reported holistically, systematically, and consistently.

Workforce development is one of those external factors or pressure points for community colleges; increasing public awareness of our nation's need to maintain its competitive edge in the global economy will demand an even more responsive and flexible workforce development and training system. Obstacles to providing more effective delivery of workforce training by community colleges will continue to raise questions about their operations, funding, delivery systems, employment qualification and compensation systems, and even the organizational structure and governance of the colleges. It is the colleges' strong record in workforce preparation and development that will keep them under the magnifying glass. Because of the criticality of this function to national security, federal funds and new programs to support workforce preparation and development will be expanded or reallocated from educational programs perceived as less effective. Eventually the transfer function may be diminished.

References

Brint, S. G., and Karabel, J. B. *The Diverted Dream.* New York: Oxford University Press, 1989.

Dougherty, K. J., and Bakia, M. F. "Community Colleges and Contract Training." *Teachers' College Record,* 2000, *102*(1), 197–243.

Education Commission of the States. *State Policies on Community College Workforce Development: Findings from a National Survey.* Denver, Colo.: Education Commission of the States, 2002.

Friedman, T. *The World Is Flat: A Brief History of the Twenty-First Century.* New York: Farrar, Straus and Giroux, 2005.

Grubb, W. N., Bell, D., Bragg, D. D., and Russam, M. *Workforce, Economic, and Community Development: The Changing Landscape of the Entrepreneurial Community College.* Berkeley, Calif.: National Center for Vocational Education, National Council for Occupational Education, 1997.

Jacobs, J., and Dougherty, K. J. "The Uncertain Future of the Community College Workforce Development Mission." In B. K. Townsend and K. J. Dougherty (eds.), *Community College Missions in the Twenty-First Century.* New Directions for Community Colleges, no. 136. San Francisco: Jossey-Bass, 2006.

McCabe, R. H., and Pincus, L. "Federal Workforce Legislation." In R. H. McCabe (ed.), *The American Community College: Nexus for Workforce Development.* Phoenix, Ariz.: League for Innovation in the Community College, 1997.

McGuinness, A. C. *Education Commission of the State's (ECS) Brief: Reflections on Postsecondary Governance Changes.* Denver, Colo.: Education Commission for the States, 2002.
National Governors Association. *Postsecondary Education Reform in Kentucky.* Washington, D.C.: National Governors Association, 2001.
Varner, J. *Forty Years of Growth and Achievement: A History of Iowa's Community Colleges.* Des Moines: Iowa Department of Education, 2006.

JANICE NAHRA FRIEDEL serves as Iowa's state director for community colleges and state director for Career and Technical Education.

NEW DIRECTIONS FOR COMMUNITY COLLEGES • DOI: 10.1002/cc

This chapter examines the role of community college governance in a P–16 environment. The discussion focuses on development of the initiative, opportunities, and challenges faced in Texas and other states that have P–16 or P–20 systems.

Closing the Gaps in Texas: The Critical Role of Community Colleges

Laurie Bricker

Calls to restructure and realign federal and statewide educational policies and programs are increasing. In March 2007, the National Governors Association published the Principles of Federal Preschool–College (P–16) Alignment. It suggested that "Congress should take this unprecedented opportunity and make every effort to align the federal education laws, as well as support state efforts to create an educational continuum from preschool through college, commonly referred to as P–16 alignment" (National Governors Association, 2007, p. 1). A recent report by the State Higher Education Executive Officers (2007) notes, "achieving the educational goals of the next generation will require policymakers and educators to view education as an integrated system, from birth through adulthood" (p. 1). Such reforms require changes in institutional governance at the local and state levels. This chapter focuses on organizational governance and best practices in Texas, with brief highlights from other states implementing P–16 systems.

The goal of the Texas Higher Education Coordinating Board (THECB) is to provide affordable, accessible, and high-quality higher education that prepares individuals for a changing economy and furthers the development and application of knowledge through instruction, research, and public service (THECB, 2004). The THECB's mission is to work with the legislature, governor, governing boards, and higher education institutions to provide the people of Texas the widest access to higher education in the most efficient manner. The THECB was initially formed by the Texas Legislature in

NEW DIRECTIONS FOR COMMUNITY COLLEGES, no. 141, Spring 2008 © 2008 Wiley Periodicals, Inc.
Published online in Wiley InterScience (www.interscience.wiley.com) • DOI: 10.1002/cc.315

1965. Currently the board is composed of nine governor-appointed members who serve for staggered six-year terms.

The THECB establishes state higher education plans, coordinates degree programs, and administers state and federal programs. The THECB hosts training for university regents and board members annually and mentors them in governance of their universities. Conferences held throughout the year highlight successes as well as intense discussions of challenges faced throughout the state. The Coordinating Board's role is guidance and policymaking to and for all public institutions of higher education, and to a much lesser extent independent colleges and universities that operate primarily through private funding and tuition.

There are distinctions between the governance, oversight, and goal setting done for community colleges and that done for four-year institutions. Whereas all public four-year university, state, and technical college regents are appointed by the governor, community and junior college trustees are elected by their local communities. In addition, all community colleges receive a majority of funding through a local tax base. The state portion of community college funding is computed from the median cost of providing instruction and administration per contact hour, rather than the more complicated matrix formula used for their four-year counterparts. Because of their elected members and local tax base, community college boards in Texas operate somewhat autonomously and tend to focus on the needs of the local district and the constituencies that elected them.

In 2000 the THECB adopted an ambitious goal, which has since become the state's comprehensive plan called Closing the Gaps by 2015 (2007). The goals and strategies provide benchmarks that include increasing the number of students enrolled in college, increasing the number of students who persist, strengthening the reputation of the colleges through nationally recognized programs, and increasing the level of federal science and engineering research funding. These four critical components of Closing the Gaps are considered essential if the state of Texas is to compete in a national and international economic market. However, reaching these ambitious goals lies squarely on the shoulders of community colleges. The governance of community colleges, their vision, and their leadership will determine the fate of higher education in Texas within the next few years.

The Urgency

The critical goal in the Closing the Gaps by 2015 plan lies with participation: over 630,000 new students are to be added to the already 1.1 million students enrolled currently in higher education throughout Texas. The THECB estimates that 70 percent of these students will begin their studies in Texas public two-year institutions. Consequently, community colleges need to ensure that they have the facilities and programs necessary to accommodate this expansion.

NEW DIRECTIONS FOR COMMUNITY COLLEGES • DOI: 10.1002/cc

Because community colleges play a pivotal role in the linkage between graduating high school students and those going to college, P–16 efforts have emerged across the state. As a result of the state's 79th Legislative Session, the alignment of curriculum that ensures smooth transition of high school graduates to college is now law. House Bill 1 (2006) from that session mandates instructional rigor and alignment of courses to college expectations. In short, this law mandates communication between K–12 and higher education institutions. No longer is it acceptable for K–12 educational leaders to work in educational silos, isolated from their higher education counterparts who also work in their own silos. Once again the critical responsibility to ensure this success lies squarely on the shoulders of the community colleges, where the bulk of high school graduates throughout the state are expected to enter higher education.

The Problem

Several recent events have created major stumbling blocks for the community colleges responsible for providing greater access to the state's graduating high school seniors, and governance appears to be a factor in each event.

North Harris Montgomery Community College (NHMCC), with an enrollment of 45,000 in credit courses and 13,000 in continuing education courses, has had a stable and competent board, chancellor, and campus presidents. However, in 2006 NHMCC lost a critical bond election and an opportunity for annexation, both of which would have enabled the college district to build facilities and expand its tax base. In addition, two seasoned board members lost their seats during the election. In May 2007 a new chancellor was elected on a split six-to-three board vote, an outward showing of division among the NHMCC board members. The question thus becomes, How will a divided board with new administrative leadership come together to face a courageous challenge of passing both a much-needed bond election and annexation?

Houston Community College System, with an enrollment of 50,000 students, is also restricted in district size and tax base. This restriction can be lifted only by initiating an annexation to include current unaffiliated areas in the greater Houston area, including Katy, North Forest, Alief, and Spring Branch. All these (except North Forest) are in separate school districts and do not pay community college taxes. In 2004 some business communities encouraged the Houston Community College (HCC) board to hold an annexation vote that would include the currently taxed district's votes in the four proposed annexation areas. An outcry of taxation without representation emerged, with the four proposed areas' leadership storming HCC board meetings and urging the HCC board to rescind their vote. Tempers flared, board members were lobbied and coerced, procedural points made, and executive sessions were conducted. After numerous meetings and protracted discussions, the board majority voted to postpone the annexation discussion indefinitely. Currently there are no formal plans to conduct the four annexation votes so critical to reaching the goals of the Closing the Gaps by 2015 plan.

However, the question remains: How will Houston Community College—or any community college—expand to meet the needs of Closing the Gaps? Annexation of outlying districts may mean that current board members will not be reelected to the board. Furthermore, taxpayers in the areas proposed for annexation will expect assurances of fair representation on the board. They will also have to be convinced that paying taxes to the college district will benefit them and their families in the end. These concerns must be addressed before a successful annexation will occur in Houston or anywhere in Texas.

Unfortunately critical board elections taking place at Houston Community College in November 2007 went largely ignored. The business community that previously had taken a leadership position in elections was virtually silent. A critical seat was vacated by a leader who faced a lawsuit over his campaign financing; no one from the business community got involved. And as in many U.S. metropolitan areas, "down-ballot" issues were overlooked as voters addressed ballot measures that appeared more important. It is possible, therefore, for the leadership of community colleges to become elected with little consideration of the candidates' background, capabilities, or intent.

The Challenge

Whether the THECB or local leadership is at the helm, countless conferences and conventions are held throughout the state each year. P–16 is a frequent topic of conversation and a focus of each conference. During conference proceedings, business leaders often speak on the economic consequences if Texas does not meet Closing the Gaps goals—namely, the state will not measure up economically compared to other states in the nation (THECB, 2007). P–12 board members and administrators participate in these conferences along with leaders from the higher education sector.

Time and again observers lament the lack of rigor of graduating seniors, the uneven quality of academic courses compared across high schools, and the fact that 40 to 60 percent of entering college freshmen require developmental or remedial classes. There is also concern that poor, first-generation, and minority students make up the majority of the large urban K–12 districts' population. Many of these students are not completing high school at acceptable levels, and accurate predictors of attrition have not been developed. Furthermore, the state is grappling with the realization that passing the state-required Texas Assessment of Knowledge and Skills (TAKS) test is not a reliable predictor of college success for those who do complete high school and enter college.

To address all these challenges, community colleges need to reach out to high schools, break out of the silos of education and information, and forge partnerships that will ensure acceptable high school completion, workforce training, dual credit courses, and a smoother transition into the world of college. To date, efforts to close the gaps in Texas have led to pockets of educational excellence around the state. This situation should be viewed as an opportunity for community college reform—for both community colleges and leadership in the state.

Pockets of Excellence

Every year the THECB recognizes higher education initiatives that document excellence in the areas of participation, success, excellence, or research known as the Star Awards (THECB, 2006). Eligible programs must have been operational for at least two years and be replicable. Following is one such success.

Austin Community College. The Austin Community College (ACC) district is having great success in its P–16 initiatives. Each year the board and president establish institutional priorities that are then linked to the college's planning, evaluation, and resource allocation models. The board also hosts several community forums throughout the year with groups such as regional chambers of commerce and community-based organizations to hear their needs and their assessment of college responsiveness. These values are important in establishing an institutional culture of collaboration, responsiveness, and accountability.

An example of the success is ACC's College Connection program, which provides a series of structured activities and services for high school students to receive one-on-one assistance applying to ACC and for financial aid. All services are delivered by college staff on the high school campuses. High school graduates receive their diploma and also are ready to register at ACC by phone or web. Many of the participants leave the programs with ACC Early College Start dual credit. Awarded a Texas Higher Education Coordinating Board Star Award and the Bellwether Award, the program has expanded to serve twenty-two school districts in the ACC service area and has attracted a substantial amount of external funding to help it grow. It also has been adopted by several other Texas colleges.

San Jacinto College. San Jacinto College North has established a nationally recognized developmental education program through certification by the National Association of Developmental Education. Innovative teaching, implementation of new policy based on research, and a supportive administration were not enough to bring students to college readiness in a short span of time. It was apparent that the college needed to start to dialogue with the high schools, especially in mathematics. During the summer of 2006, the Galena Park, Channelview, and Sheldon school districts sent a group of their math teachers to work with the math developmental education instructors at San Jacinto College North. This has led to a new dialogue between the college instructors and the high school math teachers. Over the summer they will examine the outcomes of this project and how can they assist each other in making that transition smoother. The magic of this project is that the faculty realized they had the same issue and they needed to move forward to help each other solve that issue.

South Texas College. South Texas College (STC) understands that community colleges play a critical role in creating a strong P–16 environment. Thus, STC has undertaken many initiatives to meet three critical goals: increase college attendance rates, increase college readiness, and increase college degree completion.

South Texas College has partnered with seven high schools in four school districts to sponsor one-day events to facilitate the financial aid and admissions process for college-bound high school seniors. The partnership between South Texas College, the University of Texas–Pan American, and Mission Consolidated Independent School District began this strategy with the goal of ensuring that every high school senior complete a college application and apply for financial aid.

The board of trustees at STC continues to demonstrate its commitment to access by waiving tuition and fees for dual enrollment students. Because lack of money is the greatest deterrent for potential dual enrollment students, this step required courage. The board determined that maintaining this priority has increased dual enrollment from approximately four hundred high school students to over 4,500 students. The college has also recognized the need to expand the early college opportunities for high school students who demonstrate readiness to pursue a more rigorous program while still enrolled in high school. STC therefore created the Dual Enrollment Medical Science Academy and the Dual Enrollment Engineering Academy, which offer associate of science degrees in biology and engineering.

Houston Community College. In 2003 a collaborative effort between Houston Community College–Southwest's West Loop Campus and Houston Independent School District began intending to offer to a specific student population the opportunity to earn college credit while still attending high school. According to the Early College Initiative Program's web site, this program focuses on "students for whom a smooth transition into postsecondary education is now problematic" (Jobs for the Future, 2007).

In July 2003 the Houston Independent School District, Houston Community College System, and Houston A+ Challenge jointly created the Challenge Early College High School. This unique school is specifically designed to give students the opportunity to begin college after the tenth or during the eleventh grade. The school redefines the typical comprehensive high school experience in a small school setting housed on a community college campus. Students in this program can accelerate progress from the ninth grade through the first two years of college in five years, earning the associate of arts degree. In three years, the Challenge Early College High School program has enabled fifteen of forty-six high school graduates to acquire their associate degrees, while the entire group graduated with an average of forty-five transferable college-level credits per student.

NEW DIRECTIONS FOR COMMUNITY COLLEGES • DOI: 10.1002/cc

P–16 programs are springing up everywhere across the state. With support and encouragement from the THECB, and field specialists salaried by the THECB's foundation, there are new and budding P–16s in Austin, Houston, Tyler, and San Antonio. Through the leadership of THECB board members and community, business, and education leaders, new ideas for additional P–16s are being generated. Developing a prototype and with strong support from THECB staff, board members charged into communities to identify leadership, organize meetings, and lead the development of desperately needed conversation, convocations, and action. Thus far, each P–16 is beginning to flourish and serve as a catalyst for other new and emerging councils. Galvanizing and committing community leadership could not have been accomplished without the leadership of the THECB board.

El Paso. The El Paso Collaborative for Academic Excellence, founded in 1991 and based at the University of Texas–El Paso (UTEP), sends mentors into public elementary, middle, and high schools to work closely with teachers on curriculum development and improved teaching methods. Schools participating in the El Paso program have seen substantial improvements in minority students' test scores in math and reading (UTEP, 2007). The gap between the passing rate for non-Hispanic white students and their African American and Hispanic peers on those tests has been closing. For example, "in 1992–93, just 32.3 percent of African American and 36.2 percent of Hispanic students achieved passing scores on the math portion of TAAS [the state's mandatory high school exit test prior to the TAKS]—barely more than half the 63.1 percent passing rate achieved by white students. By 2001–02, passing rates had climbed dramatically for all students and were fewer than eight percentage points apart: 87 percent for African American, 89.2 percent for Hispanic and 94.9 percent for white students" (UTEP, 2007).

Houston Independent School District and Spring Branch Independent School District. During the last two years both the Houston Independent School District (the largest district in the state) and the Spring Branch Independent School District (ISD) have announced their college-bound culture goals. In both districts, this push originated and was led by the district's board of education. Both districts are focused and working fervently to align curriculum, collaborate with neighboring community colleges and universities, and make it known to the public that all students in their districts will be college ready when they graduate from their high schools. Both districts' missions were board-driven and board-led. In the Houston Independent School District every piece of stationery features a college-bound logo and clearly states the district's intent that every one of their students be college ready.

The Spring Branch ISD community has high expectations for educational excellence in their schools. To meet those expectations, the board first examined its values and developed a statement of core commitments that would guide the goals of a Five-Year Educational Plan (2006–2011). Spring Branch ISD also hired a dedicated college counselor for each high school to support these efforts. Their mission is to advance the district's college-focused goal and support individual students in reaching their goal of going to college.

Finally, the Greater Houston P–16+ Council was formed in 2005 to emphasize that the entire region is responsible for the effort, and the goal reaches beyond a baccalaureate degree. Having cohosted and sponsored conferences and counseled with P–16s across the state, the Greater Houston P16+ Council stands poised to serve as a P–16 model for the nation overall.

Other states have had or are developing their own initiatives. According to the Education Commission of the States (2006), there are currently thirty states actively involved in P–16 initiatives. While one state, Florida, enacted a governance change, most states have taken an incremental approach to implementing a P–16 system. Five states (Florida, Indiana, North Carolina, Ohio, and Texas) have passed legislation to establish a P–16 council or initiative, but most are formed voluntarily or through executive order. A sixth state, Delaware, created its P–16 council through executive order, then enacted legislation to codify it into law. Most P–16 councils have business and community involvement.

One outstanding model is Georgia's Postsecondary Readiness Enrichment Program, or PREP, which helps middle students better understand college expectations through mentoring, field trips to colleges, and other activities. Some 45,000 students in two hundred middle schools have participated. Georgia also established the nation's first state and local network of P–16 councils, which help coordinate activities at colleges and public schools.

The Future

Walking the walk and talking the talk will be the true measures of future community college success. Clearly, community colleges will be the focal point of Closing the Gaps by 2015—in Texas as in all other states. Success in the next eight years will be measured by the ability of community colleges to educate significantly more students, provide support for high school alignment, college readiness, dual credit, and transition, both from high schools and to four-year universities. These abilities can be viewed as a burden by some taxpayers in community college districts, causing anti-tax candidates to run and win board seats. Conversely, many taxpayers will consider these expanded community college services a boon to the economic health of the college district, the state, and the nation. Corporate leaders and community college boards and administrators must focus on the critical economic and instructional roles of two-year colleges. P–16 councils will continue to play an integral role in keeping the focus on priorities and open communication among all participants. Fortunately, the THECB, institutional governing boards, and civic leaders now recognize that existing pockets of excellence in the state must be extended to an excellent statewide system. The economic future of Texas and the entire nation depends on it.

References

Education Commission of the States. *P–16 Collaboration in the States*. Denver, Colo.: Education Commission of the States, 2006.

House Bill 1. Third Called Session, 79th Texas Legislature. Texas State Legislature, 2006.

Jobs for the Future. *Early College Initiative Program*. Boston: Jobs for the Future, 2007.

National Governors Association. *Principles of Federal Preschool–College (P–16) Alignment*. Washington, D.C.: National Governors Association, 2007.

State Higher Education Executive Officers. *More Student Success: A Systematic Solution*. Boulder, Colo.: State Higher Education Executive Officers, 2007.

Texas Higher Education Coordinating Board. *Agency Strategic Plan for Fiscal Years 2005–2009*. Austin: Texas Higher Education Coordinating Board, 2004.

Texas Higher Education Coordinating Board. *The Texas Higher Education Star Award*. Austin: Texas Higher Education Coordinating Board, 2006.

Texas Higher Education Coordinating Board. *Closing the Gaps by 2015*. Austin: Texas Higher Education Coordinating Board, 2007.

University of Texas at El Paso. *El Paso Collaborative for Academic Excellence: Who We Are*. El Paso: University of Texas at El Paso, 2007.

LAURIE BRICKER serves as a board member of the Texas Higher Education Coordinating Board.

NEW DIRECTIONS FOR COMMUNITY COLLEGES • DOI: 10.1002/cc

This chapter offers a three-nation perspective on college governance, emphasizing the condition of autonomy embedded in governance arrangements.

Yanks, Canucks, and Aussies: Governance as Liberation

John S. Levin

Underlying the goals and actions of colleges and universities is the practice of governance. Theoretically, governance comprises both a system of regulations and the pattern of behaviors of those who make decisions about the institution's functioning. This pattern emanates from the foundational values that organize the institution. Yet governance in higher education is difficult to comprehend in the abstract or without observation of the practice itself. While customarily viewed as a system of formal and informal decision making, and a structure that reflects authority and hierarchy, governance also pertains to relationships both within an institution and between the institution and other entities, such as government, business, and the public (Marginson and Considine, 2000).

Governance is part of a historical and cultural process that both reflects and shapes institutional identity. Institutions are both agents and recipients of change, altering their social, cultural, and political contexts and being altered by these contexts. In the public sphere, government has primacy of authority for institutions. While governments have authority to change governance processes and structures in colleges, such changes do not emerge from thin air or within government, but from the negotiated order between government and its institutions and from the social, political, and economic context in which government operates in any given jurisdiction. The relationships between government and institution are one focus for the examination and understanding of governance. One outcome

DISCOVER SOMETHING GREAT

NEW DIRECTIONS FOR COMMUNITY COLLEGES, no. 141, Spring 2008 © 2008 Wiley Periodicals, Inc.
Published online in Wiley InterScience (www.interscience.wiley.com) • DOI: 10.1002/cc.316

of these relationships is the legislation that regulates and guides institutions. Such legislation exists within a particular context.

I offer an international perspective to demonstrate institutional contexts and the ways in which they shape governance in community colleges, as well as to explain governance as a dynamic and multilayered process. Though limited to three countries—the United States, Canada, and Australia—this perspective serves to exemplify alternate cultural, social, and political contexts for higher or postcompulsory education. On the one hand, the three countries and their citizens—Yanks, Canucks, and Aussies—share colonial roots and the English language. On the other hand, their postcolonial histories have diverged as a consequence of many factors, including geography, climate, immigration demographics, religion, and aboriginal and native peoples, among others (Barman, 1991; Lipset, 1989; MacIntyre, 2004). Furthermore, their colleges, institutes, and universities have taken on different characteristics, making the comparison of some institutional types problematic because of vast discrepancies among the countries' institutional structures and purposes. For example, the private research university of the United States is without precedent in Canada and almost negligible in Australia, with only two minor institutions so categorized. The university colleges of British Columbia in Canada—a hybrid of the open access community college and four-year public college—are not found in other countries.

Furthermore, the rapid changes taking place nationally and globally in postsecondary education create another comparative problem. Does the comparison look at institutions in the present, in the past, or both? For example, the university colleges of British Columbia were, prior to 1989, public or community colleges. As university colleges, they still retain much of their community college character, including those defining principles of a community college such as open access and a comprehensive curriculum (Dennison, 2000; Levin, 2001b, 2003). At the same time, they are arguably different institutional types in 2007 from what they were prior to 1989. The history of Technical and Further Education (TAFE) institutes in Australia reflects a pattern of continual reinvention and legal alterations (Anderson, 1998). Yet these institutes are the closest comparable institutions to community colleges in the United States and Canada. Although they emphasize vocational training, TAFE institutes possess community college features such as open access, a wide array of education and training programs, and student transfer (Goozee, 2001). Finally, the U.S. community college is not one homogenous entity, with colleges in some jurisdictions reflecting the traditional junior college image—preparation for transfer to a university— and others decidedly favoring a vocational, workforce development focus.

In this chapter I refer to the three countries' major postsecondary, nonuniversity sector as community colleges. However, I will also refer to them as they are separately known in their countries—community colleges in the United States, public colleges in Canada, and TAFE institutes in Aus-

NEW DIRECTIONS FOR COMMUNITY COLLEGES • DOI: 10.1002/cc

tralia. Because of their differing institutional identities, I will not compare them directly, but rather discuss each separately by using three related themes. These include the development of participatory governance involving faculty in institutional decision making in the United States, the development of dual authority for governance in Canada, and the permutations of institutional authority for governance in Australia.

The Jurisdictions

Within their respective nations, the state of California in the United States, the province of British Columbia in Canada, and the state of Victoria in Australia are viewed as trendsetters, bellweather jurisdictions, and even the radical chic of their nations. These jurisdictions' higher education institutions are no exception. In California the sector known as the community college provides a comprehensive curriculum, open-access admissions to a broad spectrum of courses as well as competitive entry to specialized career-oriented programs, and forms one segment of a tripartite higher education system—the largest single higher education system in the United States. In British Columbia the taxonomy is increasingly complicated: the post-secondary educational system that excludes the province's four chartered universities is referred to as colleges and university-colleges. Similar to California's community colleges, after which they were modeled (Dennison and Gallagher, 1986), these institutions have provided baccalaureate degrees since the mid-1990s. They also offer comprehensive curriculum, including developmental and vocational education, and continue to provide open access to a broad spectrum of courses. In Victoria the TAFE institutes offer students open access to nonuniversity, tertiary education and training, with particular emphasis on vocational education and training geared toward employment.

Participation Broadly Defined: The Academic Senate in California

The California community college governance story begins with Assembly Bill 1725 (1988), an omnibus bill that reputedly changed California community colleges by eroding the authority of college administrators and elevating faculty (White, 1998). The critical language for faculty elevation in governance appears in section 70902, article 7, which compels the governing board to establish procedures "to ensure faculty, staff, and students the opportunity to express their opinions at the campus level and to ensure that these opinions are given every reasonable consideration, and the right to participate effectively in district and college governance, and the right of academic senates to assume primary responsibility for making recommendations in the areas of curriculum and academic standards."

NEW DIRECTIONS FOR COMMUNITY COLLEGES • DOI: 10.1002/cc

Furthermore, the board of governors of the California community colleges was charged with developing policies and guidelines to strengthen the role of the academic senate in matters of academic and professional standards. This led to Title 5, section 53200–206, of the Education Code of California: "The governing board of a community college district shall adopt policies for the appropriate delegation of authority and responsibility to its college and district academic senate. Among other matters, said policies, at a minimum, shall provide that the governing board or its designees will consult collegially with the academic senate when adopting policies and procedures on academic and professional matters. This requirement to consult collegially shall not limit other rights and responsibilities of the academic senate which are specifically provided in statute or other regulations contained in this part." In addition, article 2 of the California Code defines senate purview and authority. Academic and professional matters comprise the following policy development and implementation matters:

- Curriculum
- Degree and certificate requirements
- Grading policies
- Educational program development
- Standards or policies governing student preparation and success
- District and college governance structures, as related to faculty roles
- Faculty roles and involvement in accreditation processes, including self-study and annual reports
- Policies for faculty professional development activities
- Processes for program review
- Processes for institutional planning and budget development
- Other academic and professional matters as mutually agreed upon between the governing board and the academic senate

Arguably, it was not the requirement of faculty participation that constituted a enhanced role for faculty in the operations of community colleges, but rather detailed requirements for the operation, management, and actions of community colleges that must rely on a formal body of faculty (Livingston, 1998). Furthermore, the bilateral nature of governance in and for California's community colleges—including individual institutions or districts and the state system as a whole—requires senate participation and de facto approval of policy on academic and professional matters (Academic Senate for California Community Colleges, 1996). Thus, while individual faculty have gained elevated status in community colleges through legal language that requires their participation in governance, a body—the faculty senate both at individual institutions and statewide—has primacy in governing board decisions on academic and professional matters.

NEW DIRECTIONS FOR COMMUNITY COLLEGES • DOI: 10.1002/cc

On the Path to Bicameral Governance: The Academy in British Columbia

By the time public or community colleges in British Columbia had reached their third decade of existence, they were not only a system under the direction of the provincial government but also potential vehicles for government public policy expanding opportunities for baccalaureate degree attainment (Levin, 1995, 2001b, 2003). Furthermore, the influence of faculty through provincial unionization and the strength of the university transfer function, in tandem with government investigations of access to baccalaureate degrees, combined to align government planning with faculty ambitions (Dennison, 1992; Levin, 1995; Levin, 1994). By the middle of the 1990s, five colleges had achieved baccalaureate degree-granting status, and all the provincial colleges were legislated to establish and run an education council, a body that verged on a second authority structure for individual colleges (Government of British Columbia, 2000; Levin, 2001a). Indeed, if board-only authority is viewed as unicameral governance, then board and faculty authority can be viewed as bicameral governance. Thus, public colleges in British Columbia were jointly governed: formally through the education council and the governing board, and informally through other mechanisms such as collective bargaining agreements and provincial government behaviors that accorded faculty a place at the table for institutional decisions.

Legislation for the education council ensures that faculty members have a 50 percent voting membership. Composition of an education council consists of twenty voting members, of which

Ten must be faculty members elected by the faculty members
Four must be students elected by the students
Two must be educational administrators appointed by the president
Two must be support staff elected by the support staff

The president is a nonvoting member of the education council.

Within institutions, the education council serves as the sole formal advisor of the governing board on educational matters. Should the board not take the council's advice, then the board must offer a justification to the council for the board's decision. An education council must advise the board, and the board must seek advice from the education council, on the development of educational policy for the following matters: mission statement, educational goals, and objectives, strategies, and priorities of the institution. Furthermore, the advice of the educational council pertains to all curricula and policies related to admissions, faculty qualifications, and the like. The council's input covers the gamut of educational and instructional behaviors of a college.

In addition to advising the board, the council has powers over student academic performance, including, for example, policies for evaluation and student appeals. Thus, on student academic matters the council is the pre-eminent authority. Finally, joint approval from the council and the board is required for such actions as determining the status of courses and programs from other institutions and from one part of the institution compared to another part (in the case of establishing equivalency). This authority is enabled through the provincial government minister, and any decisions that cannot be reached jointly are referred to the minister.

In short, the role of the education council is comprehensive in educational matters. In the authority and approval structure, the council has been established to share joint authority with the governing board on several matters and to have primacy in advising the board on those educational matters where the education council does not have joint authority.

The maintenance of this joint authority contributed not only to workers' militancy but also to governments acceding to union demands (Barman, 1991). Additionally, specific government commissions have reinforced the bicameral ethos (Plant, 2007). For example, while the latest commission recommended that colleges in British Columbia have their baccalaureate degree–granting status rescinded, the commission has been silent on the bicameral nature of governance in those colleges. Silence in this case reflects acceptance of the practice. Even with neoliberal orientations, provincial governments since the late 1980s in British Columbia have clung to social democratic sentiments, couching their economic and political goals in language that engenders social cohesion and equality (Province of British Columbia Ministry of Education Skills and Training, 1996). Thus, governance of British Columbia's colleges is consistent with principles of equity, and faculty have an equal if not a dominant role in the functioning of colleges.

Released from the State: Institutional Detachment in Victoria and South Australia

Whereas self-governing institutions are viewed as both necessary and part of the progressive evolution of TAFE institutes in Victoria (Thomas, 2000), self-governance became soundly criticized as corporatization in South Australian TAFEs and ultimately ended in favor of a unified state system of networked institutions (Kirby, Ryan, and Carter, 2002). While Victoria favored autonomy, particularly from government, South Australia favored the government–public service arrangement. For South Australia, institutional detachment from government led to deteriorating performance and negative outcomes of TAFE (Kirby, Ryan, and Carter, 2002); for Victoria, TAFE autonomy has been praised (TAFE Directors of Australia, 2007; Thomas, 2000).

Australia's TAFEs—Technical and Further Education institutes— occupy a rather complex position in education in Australia. Although the national policy framework for vocational education and training is jointly negotiated and managed by the national government and state and territory governments, the states and territories have legal and financial responsibility for TAFE institutes. As the national preeminence of TAFE expands along with a national policy agenda for skills development and vocational education, the responsibilities for meeting national policy objectives fall upon the states and territories (Goozee, 2001). The historical tensions between the national government and the state or territorial governments are particularly evident in the development of TAFE. As neoliberal policies have taken hold globally, national pressures for global competition steer institutions toward economic markets, often at the expense of local and social needs (Anderson, 2006; Marginson, 1993). The loosening of government formal ties, particularly in the bureaucratic control of decisions and operations, points toward liberalizing practices of the state, but it also leads to economic competition among the players, neglect of government social policies, and greater accountability of public institutions. While autonomy from the state can be viewed as freedom from control, such autonomy can also be seen as a struggle for institutional survival. Thus, while Victoria's TAFEs gained autonomy in institutional governance, South Australia, which already had such autonomy, gave it up. For South Australia, TAFE autonomy led to disappointing outcomes for communities and to dysfunctional resource management (Kirby, Ryan, and Carter, 2002). For Victoria, autonomy was only partial, as the TAFEs depended primarily on public finances for operations, but nonetheless self-governance permitted institutional flexibility and reputed responsiveness to both local communities and industries.

By law, Victoria's TAFEs are legally autonomous from government in their operations. Their governing body—councils—are incorporated and have legislative authority to oversee and manage the college directly, including oversight for courses and programs. Legislatively, the council is responsible for the performance of TAFE colleges. Yet they are accountable to the government, and 50 percent of council members are appointed by the government minister. Councils appoint a director as chief executive officer and may delegate powers to the director. Such a structure permits at least arm's-length distance from government and considerable autonomy for TAFE colleges, but it does not detach these institutions from government and raises the possibility of conflicts or tensions over institutional purposes.

After a decade of corporate status, Victoria's TAFEs were judged as both social institutions and as businesses with strong entrepreneurial orientations, but the emphasis was on economic development, employment growth, and national competitiveness (Noonan, 2002). In such an orientation, TAFEs may have ignored social policy issues and neglected their social role, which includes promoting social cohesion through second-chance education and equity programs and supporting local and regional communities affected by structural economic and technological change. In other words, in addressing government economic policy, these institutions may struggle to address social policy as well.

Yet the balancing acts between government instruments of economic and social policy and between autonomous institution and handmaiden of the state are evident. The specifications for Victoria TAFEs on the state level apply to TAFEs nationally as well. "On the one hand, government expects TAFE institutes to provide standardized public education to Victorian citizens and industry. On the other hand, it expects them to be flexible to the needs of their local communities and to be commercially competitive—that is, to be more like private businesses" (Thomas, 2000). Clearly, TAFE is an instrument of the state, whether it has detached itself from government to become a corporate, self-governing body or not.

College Governance and the State

Governments alone are not the sole arbiters of community college governance; in some U.S. jurisdictions, governments accede a substantial portion of their authority either to institutions or to coordinating or governing bodies. When this devolution of authority occurs in a state with no unionized institutions, then considerable authority resides at the individual institutional level, in the hands of boards and presidents. The state of Arizona is a salient, if not an extreme, example, where the absence of both state government oversight and a weak or recently disestablished state governing board and a nonunionized faculty workforce together correspond with individual institutions' functioning under the directives of the governing board and the president of the college. This condition is not unlike that in the state of Victoria, Australia, where legal authority has devolved from government to institutions, but there government oversight is maintained. Similarly, in British Columbia, Canada, government oversight is entrenched in legislation, but considerable authority has devolved to institutions. Unlike public universities in these three countries, community colleges in the United States, Canada, and Australia are ultimately responsible to the state, and autonomy is not a formal condition of their legal existence. The state may alter conditions of institutional operations and institutional life either by legislation or by retracting delegated authority. Thus, governance of community colleges tends to operate within a political framework, including the negotiated order between government and its institutions and the social, political, and economic context within which government operates in any given jurisdiction. In California we see the development of faculty senate prominence, not institutional prominence, in governing both individual colleges and the state's community college system. In British Columbia, we see the increasing influence of faculty in the governance of their own individual institutions. In Victoria, Australia, we see the development of institutional autonomy (and in South Australia, the retraction of autonomy) and the prominence of councils or governing boards and directors or chief executive officers.

From this international perspective, we can see that governance develops as a form of liberation for colleges and their players. Such liberation may be in the form of separation from control by traditional structures. The California community college and the state's community college system have been revised to transfer authority to faculty senates from the traditional structures of college administration, college governing boards, the state governing board, and the state system chief executive officer. The British Columbia community college has evolved to a condition approximating bicameral governance, with faculty gaining influence at the expense of the college's administration. The Victoria college, or TAFE, has achieved corporate status, loosening itself from the dictates of the state government and responding much more to business, industry, and local community pressures. Evidently, the negotiated order has shifted so that community colleges or their players—in the form of governing boards or councils in Australia, faculty in British Columbia, and faculty senates in California—have gained power relative to the state. In spite of this apparent liberation, these colleges remain arms of the state, and ultimate authority resides with the state.

The three patterns of development of governance in these jurisdictions mirror to some extent the historical contexts of the three countries and the three specific states or provinces within these countries. Though it is perceived as a highly regulated state, individual rights in California are protected against state control, as in all U.S. states. Such an ethos extends to higher education institutions that prize autonomy for public universities and local authority for community colleges. British Columbia, while consistent with Canadian federalism, has a strong provincial government responsible for its educational institutions. Yet the evolution of the province's colleges (Dennison and Gallagher, 1986; Levin, 1995)—initiated by the University of British Columbia—suggests strong provincial direction and financing on the one hand and an emerging influence of professional educators on the other hand, including the provincewide faculty bargaining unit and administrator and board associations. Like the other states in Australia, Victoria is managed by the government, with government oversight over universities at the federal level and over TAFE at the state level.

The Larger Perspective: Local Governance and Global Implications

All three systems developed in the context of federal systems of government, and the nation-specific differences have shaped the institutional framework for systems of governance in particular ways in each jurisdiction. This is especially evident in the distribution of powers and responsibilities between national and state or provincial levels and agencies of government for U.S. community colleges, Canada's public colleges, and Australia's TAFEs. These tertiary education providers tend to be viewed as agents of state-territory-provincial government policy and are located closer, and are ostensibly more responsive, to their local communities and economies than other sectors of higher education.

All three systems emerged in the 1960s and early 1970s: in California, heralded in the Master Plan; in British Columbia, initiated by the

MacDonald Commission; and in Victoria, identified in the national Kangan Report. As such, they would all appear to reflect a global trend (in western democracies) toward massification of tertiary or postsecondary education. Specifically, they can be seen as political accommodations to relieve the mounting pressure on state and provincial finances for higher education in an era of increasing enrollments in secondary schools and rising credentialism in the labor market, leading in turn to rapidly growing demand for access to advanced education and training. As such, they are also arguably early manifestations of nation states' responses to emerging forces of globalization and have since become central tools of the nation state. While Yanks, Canucks, and Aussies have their special characteristics in institutional governance, they are both reactors to government structures in their efforts to gain autonomy or influence at the local level and agents of government policy in the development of a workforce in the context of global competition.

Implications for Practitioners

The role of government in community college governance cannot be underestimated: state, provincial, and territorial governments are the formal creators of public colleges and the bodies that can alter governance arrangements. Nonetheless, local contexts are not to be overlooked. Interpretations of legislation and government policy give rise to particular institutional behaviors. In California interpretations by numerous college faculty and administrators suggested that institutional governance was "shared" or jointly carried out by faculty and administrators (White, 1998). Governance in California community colleges was viewed as shared governance, even though Assembly Bill 1725 never used the word *shared*, indicating instead that faculty were participants in governance (Levin, 2000).

From an international perspective, it is evident that colleges and college members seek autonomy, and the entity they seek autonomy from is government. At a minimum, presidents and boards want control over their institutions, whereas faculty seek authority in academic and faculty matters. Once government has granted that authority to these parties, they must work out or negotiate a suitable and functional arrangement. It is in this relationship that tensions seem most heightened and the parties pressed to perform at optimal levels. At times they may long for the intervention of government or hark back to the bucolic days when they could fault government for their troubles.

References

Academic Senate for California Community Colleges. *The Curriculum Committee: Role, Structure, Duties, and Standards of Good Practice.* Sacramento: Academic Senate for California Community Colleges, 1996.

Anderson, D. "Chameleon or Phoenix: The Metamorphosis of TAFE." *Australian and New Zealand Journal of Vocational Education Research,* 1998, 6(2), 1–44.

Anderson, D. *Trading Places: The Impact and Outcomes of Market Reform in Vocational Education and Training.* Adelaide, Aust.: National Centre for Vocational Education Research, 2006.

Assembly Bill 1725. Sacramento, Calif., Sept. 19, 1988.

Barman, J. *The West Beyond the West: A History of British Columbia.* Toronto: University of Toronto Press, 1991.

Dennison, J. "The University-College Idea: A Critical Analysis." *The Canadian Journal of Higher Education,* 1992, 22(1), 109–124.

Dennison, J. "Characteristics of the University College in British Columbia: Governance and Administration." Paper presented at International Conference on New Developments in Higher Education. Bermuda, Oct. 2000.

Dennison, J., and Gallagher, P. *Canada's Community Colleges.* Vancouver: University of British Columbia Press, 1986.

Goozee, G. *The Development of TAFE in Australia.* Leabrook, Aust.: National Centre for Vocational Education Research, 2001.

Government of British Columbia. *College and Institute Act.* Victoria, B.C.: Queen's Printer, 2000.

Kirby, P., Ryan, R., and Carter, D. *Report of the Review of TAFE Governance in South Australia.* Adelaide, Aust.: Department of Further Education, Employment, Science and Technology, 2002.

Levin, J. "Power in the British Columbia Community College." *B.C. Studies,* 1995, 107, 60–80.

Levin, J. "What's the Impediment? Structural and Legal Constraints to Shared Governance in the Community College." *The Canadian Journal of Higher Education,* 2000, 30(2), 87–122.

Levin, J. *Globalizing the Community College: Strategies for Change in the Twenty-First Century.* New York: Palgrave, 2001a.

Levin, J. "Public Policy, Community Colleges, and the Path to Globalization." *Higher Education,* 2001b, 42(2), 237–262.

Levin, J. "Two British Columbia University Colleges and the Process of Economic Globalization." *The Canadian Journal of Higher Education,* 2003, 33(1), 59–86.

Levin, J. S. "Change and Influence in the Community Colleges of British Columbia." *The Canadian Journal of Higher Education,* 1994, 24(1), 72–87.

Lipset, S. M. *Continental Divide: The Values and Institutions of the United States and Canada.* New York: Routledge, 1989.

Livingston, T. *History of California's AB 1725 and Its Major Provisions.* Unpublished manuscript, Laguna Nigel, Calif., 1998.

MacIntyre, S. *A Concise History of Australia.* Cambridge, U.K.: Cambridge University Press, 2004.

Marginson, S. *Education and Public Policy in Australia.* Cambridge, U.K.: Cambridge University Press, 1993.

Marginson, S., and Considine, M. *The Enterprise University: Power, Governance and Reinvention in Australia.* New York: Cambridge University Press, 2000.

Noonan, P. *The Role of TAFE: Outcomes of Consultations and Identifications of Key Issues.* East Melbourne, Aust.: Victorian Learning and Employment Skills Commission, 2002.

Plant, G. *Campus 2020. Thinking Ahead: The Report. Access and Excellence: The Campus 2020 Plan for British Columbia's Post-Secondary Education System.* Victoria, B.C.: Government of British Columbia, 2007.

Province of British Columbia Ministry of Education Skills and Training. *Charting a New Course: A Strategic Plan for the Future of British Columbia Colleges.* Victoria, B.C.: Province of British Columbia Ministry of Education Skills and Training, 1996.

TAFE Directors of Australia. *Investing in Productivity: Engaging TAFE to Accelerate*

Workforce Development and Job Participation. Canberra, Aust.: TAFE Directors of Australia, 2007.

Thomas, J. *Educational Autonomy. TAFE and Autonomy: Beyond Corporate Governance.* East Melbourne, Aust.: Victoria TAFE Association, 2000.

White, K. "Shared Governance in California." In J. S. Levin (ed.), *Organizational Change in the Community College: A Ripple or a Sea Change?* New Directions for Community Colleges, no. 102. San Francisco: Jossey-Bass, 1998.

JOHN S. LEVIN is professor of higher education and director of the California Community College Collaborative (C4) at the University of California, Riverside.

NEW DIRECTIONS FOR COMMUNITY COLLEGES • DOI: 10.1002/cc

Forces inside and outside of community colleges are changing the context for governance and mandating new and different approaches to decision making.

Governance in Strategic Context

Richard L. Alfred

In a chapter titled "Reforming Governance," Alfred and Smydra (1985) offered the following observation on governance in community colleges:

> To the experienced community college administrator, one message would seem clear: competition is on the increase among different institutions to meet the demands of a changing student population. Two-year colleges will require aggressive leadership and innovative approaches to governance if they are to maintain or increase their share of the student market. . . . The questions that must be faced by community college boards, faculty, and administrators are: To what extent will any changes or dislocations in the structure of postsecondary institutions affect governance in community colleges? How will decision makers anticipate and react to these changes? Will community colleges continue in their present form or will they extend beyond their current organization and deliver new services? Will they be selectively integrated with other sectors of education as pressure mounts for coordination in a period of austerity? [p. 200]

In retrospect, this observation was simultaneously prophetic and ill conceived. A baseball scorecard would show five hits and one out. On the mark was the idea that student needs and interests are changing, competition is on the increase, and market share is an important driver for institutions. Off the mark was the notion that community colleges could be selectively integrated with other sectors of education to quell pressures for accountability and fiscal restraint. Especially insightful, however, were the

NEW DIRECTIONS FOR COMMUNITY COLLEGES, no. 141, Spring 2008 © 2008 Wiley Periodicals, Inc.
Published online in Wiley InterScience (www.interscience.wiley.com) • DOI: 10.1002/cc.317

observations on expansion of institutional boundaries to deliver new services and the impact of structural changes within institutions on governance. The context for governance in community colleges is changing, and it is changing in ways that will have implications extending vastly beyond anything we have seen in earlier periods of institutional development.

This chapter begins with a retrospective look at governance in community colleges based on a working understanding of governance as a correlate of decision making. In its simplest form, governance is "a process for distributing authority, power, and influence in decision making among constituencies" (Alfred and Smydra, 1985, pp. 201–202). What makes inquiry into governance important, both in earlier periods and today, is the notion of forces inside and outside of colleges and their relationship to governance. What are these forces? Why are they important? And what are their implications for governance? The objective of this chapter is to answer these questions by examining the contextual conditions that affect colleges and, by extension, shape the context for governance, including forces in the external environment, internal operating dynamics, and the imperative for growth and change.

Governance: A Retrospective Look

A useful account of the evolution of governance in community colleges from their early development in the 1950s and 1960s to the turn of the millennium was provided by Alfred (1998b). Portions of this account are presented here to show how some elements of current practice in governance are a carryover from the past in a sector of postsecondary education that is comparatively young.

In the short span of forty years, community colleges have evolved from small organizations administered by leaders with almost unlimited authority to complex multifaceted organizations staffed principally by specialists and part-time personnel in departments and administrative units detached from the center of the organization. In the early days, presidents made decisions with a small group of administrators and relied on an informal network to communicate the results of the decision process. As institutions grew in size and complexity, a pyramid structure for governance evolved in which power flowed from the president at the top of the organization through layers of vice presidents or deans, directors and department heads, and faculty and staff (Alfred and Carter, 1993). The allocation of resources in the budget came to be the primary mechanism of control for many presidents. Faculty maintained primary responsibility for decisions on courses, curricula, and matters pertaining to teaching and learning, and administrators maintained responsibility for decisions related to operations, priorities for institutional development, and resource allocation (Alfred, 1998b). The result was the beginning of conflict between faculty and administrators over roles in decision making. Issues were weighed in terms of their impact on stakeholders, and growing numbers of staff made the availability of resources a critical factor in decision making.

Tightening resources and increasing pressure for inclusion in decision making altered the context for governance in the late 1970s and early 1980s. Collective bargaining entered the picture, and community colleges that had assigned a primary decision-maker role to the president in their developmental years found themselves besieged by special interests. New actors outside of institutional walls laid claim to a stake in governance, including coordinating boards, legislators, local politicians, policymakers, and influential citizens (Alfred and Smydra, 1985). Few issues generated more controversy than the control of colleges and the location of power for making decisions. A sharp increase in support from the state was accompanied by state-level monitoring, auditing, and policies that affected the programs and operations of most colleges (Alfred, 1998a). At the same time, faculty and staff began to push for meaningful involvement in decision making under the banner of shared governance. Increasingly cognizant of the fact that collective bargaining could safeguard or improve working conditions, but could not guarantee involvement in strategic decisions, faculty began to establish alliances with special interest groups to push for a voice in governance. Legislation spurring a move from participative to shared governance in California community colleges ushered in a new era of governance in which words such as empowerment were routinely used by faculty and staff to describe a preferred way of doing business.

The context for governance took a corporate turn in the 1990s, when rapidly changing conditions inside and outside of colleges rendered traditional structures and systems obsolete. Students and stakeholders became more vocal in making their expectations for service and quality known and exercised other educational options when institutions responded with too little, too late. New and aggressive rivals arrived on the scene and challenged existing rules of competition by creating value for students in ways that surpassed traditional colleges. For-profit colleges brought new meaning to student intake by bringing the entire process to prospective learners at home or work, determining financial assistance on the spot, and offering lifetime placement assistance and job guarantees following program completion. Technology eliminated barriers to market entry, and a new wave of providers put a different spin on access and convenience by offering courses and services on the Internet twenty-four hours a day and seven days a week (Alfred, 2005). Finally, pressure for accountability and performance documentation intensified, as state and federal government agencies sought to gain a measure of control over costs and student outcomes.

This pressure point continues today through the work of the Spellings Commission and its efforts to push colleges and universities to do more with student access and student support. The decade of the 1990s and the early years of the new millennium changed the context for governance by encouraging approaches to decision making keyed to speed and flexibility.

The day of the slow-moving sedan on a two-lane highway was gone, and in its place was a sleek sports car on a freeway capable of accelerating quickly in response to rapidly changing conditions. On a freeway of shrinking resources and aggressive competitors, the margin for error was small: a fast-moving car could reach its destination successfully only if the driver was looking ahead.

Interestingly, the governance systems at work in community colleges today contain many of the elements of governance in earlier periods. Inside colleges, power and influence in decision making remain at the executive level, but decisions are now made by an executive team, in contrast to the president. Reliance on informal networks to interpret and communicate the why and how of decisions continues to be strong, but informal channels of communication are now a necessity to navigate the chimneys of an increasingly complex organization. Within our colleges, faculty and staff continue to push for inclusion in decision making, but the push is now more symbolic than real as the press of work created by rapidly escalating demands and diminishing full-time staff makes survival more important than engagement. Outside of colleges, pressure for accountability is escalating, but it is coming from new and different angles, some direct and some oblique, as new stakeholders holding more and varied interests get into the game.

Governance has become a process for the few and for the many; it is both an ideal and an actuality, and its meaning today is different from what it was yesterday. Depending on the importance one assigns to decision making as an imperative for improved organizational performance, governance can take on greater or lesser importance. For example, can we say with certainty that specific practices in governance actually result in better or poorer decisions? Are universal truths such as the desirability of inclusion in decision making viable under all circumstances, or only under certain circumstances? Are there automatics in governance—practices that make good sense regardless of circumstances—that should be part of every college's management arsenal? If so, what are they? I'll try to answer these questions, or at least to explore their implications for community colleges, in the pages that follow, beginning with the strategic context for governance.

Community Colleges in Strategic Context

This chapter was written in the third quarter of 2007. Anyone reading a newspaper or magazine, watching the evening news, or surfing the Internet was likely to encounter headlines focused on

- The I-35 bridge collapse in Minneapolis
- Climate change and global warming
- War or the threat of war on multiple fronts
- Terrorism and homeland security
- Declining market share for domestic automakers

NEW DIRECTIONS FOR COMMUNITY COLLEGES • DOI: 10.1002/cc

- Immigration reform
- Global competition and new economic superpowers
- Preparedness of U.S. school-age youth in a world of hypercompetition
- Declining stature of the United States in world opinion
- Presidential candidates jockeying for advantage
- Rising oil prices and calls for synthetic fuels
- Increasing health care and infrastructure costs

These challenges are global in scope, but local in impact through their influence on the goods and services people acquire, the prices they pay, and the issues in life and work they encounter each day. Thinking globally and acting locally have never been more important for service organizations (Alfred, Shults, and Seybert, 2007). On the one hand, it is a mantra that community colleges will need to embrace as they try to maintain or increase market share in a world of new players, new rules, and ever-more demanding stakeholders— a world of disequilibrium and hypercompetition. On the other hand, it is a contextual reality that leaders will need to address as they grapple with the largely unpredictable but profound impacts that diverse staff, new digital connections, and new generations will make on their institutions. Community colleges are likely to face numerous challenges to traditional forms of governance emanating from forces and conditions outside and dynamics inside institutional walls. The forms these challenges will take and their implications for governance are described next.

External Forces. The pace of transition from an industrial economy to a knowledge economy and from a national economy to a global economy will accelerate. In the new economy, community colleges will be expected to become the hub of a supplier network of schools, colleges, for-profit providers, and business working together to prepare workers with world-class skills (Alfred, Shults, and Jaquette, forthcoming). Advancing technology and global competition will open up new industries and new jobs. Existing jobs will be reconfigured to meet changing knowledge and skill requirements, and new jobs will be created to support emerging industries. Jobs that once seemed to be a source of opportunity will disappear, and others that could not have been imagined five years ago will take their place. The workforce will become more diverse as domestic and foreign markets become important sources of skilled labor. More age generations will be represented on college campuses, and demand for postsecondary education will swell beyond capacity, prompting colleges and universities to make teaching resources and materials available to people free of charge on the Internet. Just-in-time education in small learning communities will become a preferred mode for knowledge and skill acquisition among learners.

Turning to education, large numbers of students will continue to drop out of high school before graduation, and a growing number of learners will look for alternatives to the senior year. School districts seeking to improve retention and diploma completion will pursue articulation agreements with colleges and universities that funnel students into postsecondary education at an earlier age. More students will move on to college, more than half will enroll in community colleges, and most will require remediation. These learners will enter college with advanced experience and expectations for technology. Advancing technology will separate generational groups into digital "natives" and digital "immigrants," and it will revolutionize the post-secondary education market by removing barriers to market entry for new providers and meeting learners' expectations of access to learning and services twenty-four hours a day, seven days a week.

Community colleges will move into an accountability era where government agencies—local, state, and federal—will provide a greater share of funding based on evidence of value added. Spending on education will be linked to increased accountability, as public funds tighten because of mandatory expenditures for transportation, health, and national defense. Colleges will be forced to develop new assessment strategies to qualify for funding and to maintain market share with hard-driving rivals. For-profit providers will continue to challenge community colleges, but a greater threat will come from new rules of access and convenience prompted by informal learning communities seeking flexible, low-cost educational services via the Internet and traditional students swirling among and between colleges to customize the learning experience (Alfred, Shults, and Jaquette, forthcoming). New learner generations will differ from their predecessors in important ways, most notably their tolerance of diversity, their high level of comfort with new technology, and their exposure to best practices in different types of organizations, which enable them to view institutional performance in a considerably broader context. To counteract the disruptive effects of change and competition, educational providers will seek to collaborate and work in networks, ultimately making the structure of the network more important than the administrative structure of the college.

Internal Dynamics. Organizations have a natural development cycle beginning with growth followed by maturation, stability, and then decline or renewal (Alfred, 2005). Community colleges have experienced sustained explosive growth over four decades. To enable and support growth, they have become complex organizations with expansive requirements for money, staff, technology, and facilities. Their organizational architecture has grown to encompass new program and service missions, and expert staff have been hired to perform specialized functions. To cope with more functions, more responsibilities, and more staff, colleges have distributed work processes among more people, each performing a range of functions smaller and more specialized than the staff before them. Increasing specialization has led to increasing fragmentation as organizational subcultures have grown and flourished among small numbers of staff working together to deliver a service. A new organization has emerged—one with multiple sub-organizations (departments, administrative units, and work groups) pursuing specific operating objectives within the structure of a loosely coupled

NEW DIRECTIONS FOR COMMUNITY COLLEGES • DOI: 10.1002/cc

parent organization (Alfred, Shults, and Jaquette, forthcoming). The college that started as a handful of administrators and faculty serving 1,200 students in 1968 has now become a siloed, multifaceted institution serving 12,000 students with one thousand instructors and staff (including part-time) deployed in fifty academic programs and thirty service units.

Decision making and communication in this extended organization are different in form and function from their makeup in smaller organizations. Staff working in tightly knit subcultures cope with increasing size and complexity by restricting their focus to the operating unit. For many, the work unit has displaced the institution, as their touchstone and perceptions of work are formed through the lens of the work group, not through personnel in other parts of the institution. Consensual decision making and effective communication are desirable commodities in any organization, but in this siloed organization they are elusive and beyond reach. In an earlier day, staff could resolve problems through direct contact with leaders who could fix them. Increasing size and complexity have rendered direct solutions more difficult as policies, systems, and procedures have been created to coordinate the work of staff. To get work done, community colleges now rely heavily on outsourcing and partnerships composed of people and organizations outside of institutional walls. Almost every institution is partnering with K–12 schools to dually enroll students, with employers to design and deliver customized programs, with technology firms to deliver distance education, and with government agencies to promote economic development.

On this background of increasing complexity, leaders are daily confronted with challenges of changing loyalties of faculty and staff and a diminishing span of control over the institution. Activist cultures inside the college and demanding stakeholders outside are increasingly burdening seasoned leaders. Questions are being asked by boards and stakeholders that challenge the fundamentals of leadership, management, and governance. What is the college? Is it a whole organization or a sum of parts? What can leaders do to enhance individual performance and commitment when loyalty to the work unit is stronger than loyalty to the institution? Which approaches to management and decision making work most effectively in a complex multifaceted institution?

Implications for Governance

A conceptual frame that puts an interesting cast on governance in complex service organizations like community colleges is Granovetter's (1985) theory of organizational embeddedness, in which decisions are embedded in networks of personal relationships involving leaders and staff. The structural nature of embeddedness posits a tension between *ties* that bind people together and thereby encourage cohesiveness and stability and opportunities or *holes* that encourage change and enable new ideas to gain a foothold in the organization (Burt, 1992). Organizational dynamics such as increasing size and complexity favor the development of governance

NEW DIRECTIONS FOR COMMUNITY COLLEGES • DOI: 10.1002/cc

models that facilitate dualistic approaches to decision making. Once embedded in the personal network of leader-staff relationships, these models become a source of stability and cohesion, but also a force for adaptation and change.

If we use the concept of embeddedness to describe the implications for governance of forces inside and outside of community colleges, a paradox involving simultaneously contradictory conditions emerges. The dimensions of this paradox can be described as tensions between strategic and operational approaches, vertical and lateral structures, rational consistency and sense making, and institutions and networks.

Strategic and Operational Approach. The evolution of community colleges into large-scale organizations has created a tension between forces of cohesion (dynamics holding an institution together) and fragmentation (dynamics dividing an institution into parts). Examples of the former include statements of institutional vision and priorities, core values, and uniform systems and processes. Examples of the latter include divisional plans and budgets, departmental practices and procedures, and subculture norms. The implication for governance is dualism in decision making, with faculty and staff exercising control over operational decisions and the president and executive team controlling strategic decisions. The difficulty with this scheme is that the distinction between strategic and operational is often murky, and the two decision realms bleed into one another. When this happens, senior administrators narrow their focus in decision making to operations at the expense of strategy. This pattern can be observed in the tendency to confuse strategic planning priorities with institutional strategy and to elevate the budget—an instrument of control—to a statement of priorities. The effect is to remove strategy from the table as an important decision realm in governance at a time when attention to this realm is more important than ever.

Vertical and Lateral Structure. The introduction of large numbers of expert staff to carry out specialized functions has produced parallel (and sometimes competing) decision-making structures in community colleges— one vertical and the other lateral. Silos remain the organizing framework for operational decision making related to the delivery of programs and services, but a lateral structure has emerged to assume responsibility for decision making in specialized performance arenas such as student intake, curriculum development, and assessment. Staff affiliated with lateral structures work differently from staff laboring in silos. Decision making in the lateral organization is "outside-in" rather than "inside-out," with clients clearly identified, their needs and expectations determined, and need satisfaction established as the primary objective in decision making. In contrast, decision making in silos is focused to a much greater extent on maintaining balance and minimizing the disruptive effects of change. Limited resources and short staffing encourage personnel to find shortcuts and efficiencies in decision making that often make them the primary customers of their work. The implications for governance are two-fold: the number of players and beneficiaries in governance has increased, making it more complex and difficult to manage as a process; and multiple organizations with different priorities and operating modes are at work in community colleges, making governance a pluralistic process instead of a shared venue.

Rational Consistency and Sense Making. The basis on which decisions are made creates tension in community colleges. Although leaders and practitioners have been encouraged through the writings of organizational analysts and the advice of mentors to believe that the best decisions are made through a process of rational thought using adequate information, in reality many decisions are made on the basis of insufficient information. In periods of great uncertainty, rapid change, and ambiguity, the limited and piecemeal information available to decision makers sometimes leads them in the wrong direction. Drawing a parallel between woodland firefighting and organizational leadership, Weick (1996) argues that leaders sometimes misread the context in which decisions are made. They have a tendency to rely heavily on time-tested tools and thus may fail to imagine navigating a situation without them or, worse, fail to relinquish them and explore alternative paths to a decision. Under unusual operating circumstances, leaders who spend too much time seeking information to make the best decision may channel their thinking and fail to grasp the reality of the situation at hand.

The implication for governance is a need to consider parallel systems for decision making in community colleges: one better suited for rational, data-based decision making in periods of stability and the other for sense making in periods of fast change. Parallel governance may be likened to situational decision making—an arrangement by which contradictory approaches to decision making can be employed depending on the situation. The ground rules guiding the use of different systems would be known and understood by staff, and leaders would be responsible for determining which system to use depending on their assessment of the urgency of a situation, the speed of change, the need for inclusion, and the nature of a desired outcome.

Institutions and Networks. The literature on high-performing organizations encourages the need to consider alternative pathways in governance by bringing into focus the importance of *networks*. More and more colleges are collaborating with external organizations—business and industry employers, technology providers, K–12 schools, and so forth—to control costs and improve quality in an increasingly competitive market. The network poses a challenge to governance and management, however, because it calls into question the locus of power for strategic decision making—does it reside in leaders in the institution, players in the network, or both? Community colleges in a number of states are evolving into seamless P–16 educational networks involving K–12 schools, community colleges, public universities, employers, and government agencies to facilitate educational attainment through the baccalaureate degree. The rationale for doing so is compellingly simple: the outcomes and benefits produced by networks easily exceed those produced by a college, because networks expand geometrically in relation to the resource capabilities of multiple organizations, whereas colleges are limited by the quantity and quality of their internal resources (Alfred, 1998a). Networks, therefore, are not a question of yes or no, but of when and to what extent. They will become a major force in community college operations, and they will radically alter the context for governance by injecting new and influential players into the decision process.

Navigating the Paradox

A problem frequently cited by leaders in colleges undergoing growth and change is decreased opportunity for staff involvement in decisions. Inclusion—engaging staff in decisions that establish direction for the institution—is rapidly becoming a lost skill in community college management. Yet in the full-service organizations that community colleges will need to become to serve tomorrow's learners, inclusion will be perhaps the single most important determinant of leader and institutional success. Leaders will need to find ways to prevent size and complexity from turning institutions into educational bureaucracies and dispirited workplaces. They will need to turn large organizations into small ones by reducing the scale of the administrative structure and by minimizing the isolating effect of walls and boundaries. Most importantly—and this is the key to navigating the paradox of contradictory conditions—they will need to craft models for governance that engage staff in the strategic life of the institution by involving them in decisions.

It has been my practice as a thinker and writer to close articles and books with a call for change—something that will make a difference in what practitioners think and do and how institutions perform. I will forgo that practice in this chapter and instead offer an example of how governance can be modeled around a principle of inclusion using the Six Sigma program of Illinois Central College (ICC).

Developed in 1987 by Motorola, Six Sigma is a process improvement methodology used by organizations to improve performance by comparing results to customer-constituent expectations. Beginning in 2005 and continuing today, Illinois Central has incorporated Six Sigma methodology into governance by selecting and training staff to work full-time with institutional teams charged with identifying and solving institutional problems and improving business processes. The teams are cross-functional in composition and employ a methodology known as DMAIC—or define, measure, analyze, improve, and control—to identify and solve problems. Currently, more than half of the full-time faculty and staff at ICC are working on teams engaged in improving processes such as advisement, financial aid, and assessment of student performance. By engaging faculty and staff in collective problem solving using an accepted and widely practiced industry technique, Illinois Central has tackled the problem of inclusion. Decisions are made by faculty and staff working directly with customers and constituents,

NEW DIRECTIONS FOR COMMUNITY COLLEGES • DOI: 10.1002/cc

not senior administrators working apart from customers in the comfortable security of offices.

References

Alfred, R. L. "Redesigning Community Colleges to Compete for the Future." *Community College Journal of Research and Practice,* 1998a, 22(4), 315–333.

Alfred, R. L. *Shared Governance in Community Colleges: A Policy Brief Created for the Education Commission of the States.* Denver: Education Commission of the States, 1998b.

Alfred, R. L. *Managing the Big Picture in Colleges and Universities: From Tactics to Strategy.* Westport, Conn.: Praeger, 2005.

Alfred, R. L., and Carter, P. N. "Rethinking the Business of Management." In R. L. Alfred and P. N. Carter (eds.), *Changing Managerial Imperatives.* New Directions for Community Colleges, no. 84. San Francisco: Jossey-Bass, 1993.

Alfred, R. L., Shults, C., and Jaquette, O. *Community Colleges on the Horizon: Challenge, Choice, or Abundance?* Westport, Conn.: Praeger, forthcoming.

Alfred, R. L., Shults, C., and Seybert, J. *Core Indicators of Effectiveness for Community Colleges.* (3rd ed.) Washington, D.C.: Community College Press, 2007.

Alfred, R. L., and Smydra, D. F. "Reforming Governance: Resolving Challenges to Institutional Authority." In W. Deegan and D. Tillery (eds.), *Renewing the American Community College.* San Francisco: Jossey-Bass, 1985.

Burt, R. S. *Structural Holes: The Social Structure of Competition.* Cambridge, Mass.: Harvard University Press, 1992.

Granovetter, M. S. "Economic Action and Social Structure: The Problem of Embeddedness." *American Journal of Sociology,* 1985, 91(3), 481–510.

Weick, K. E. "Drop Your Tools: An Allegory for Organizational Studies." *Administrative Science Quarterly,* 1996, 41(2), 301–313.

RICHARD L. ALFRED *is professor of higher education at the University of Michigan and founding director of the Center for Community College Development.*

NEW DIRECTIONS FOR COMMUNITY COLLEGES • DOI: 10.1002/cc

9

This chapter offers a selection of references and resources on structures, processes, and outcomes of community college governance.

Key Resources on Community College Governance

Pam Schuetz

Shaped by a complex array of historic, social, economic, and political forces, the governance of America's community colleges stands apart from that of public universities as well as from public primary and secondary schools. There is no single dominant form of community college governance—it is virtually a state-by-state choice with some of the variations being state versus local control, elected versus state or locally appointed board members, taxing authority versus no taxing authority, voluntary shared governance versus mandated shared governance, and various combinations thereof. However, most literature on campus governance comes from the study of university systems and does not describe the characteristics and dynamics of community college governance (Cohen and Brawer, 2003).

Community college governance involves structures similar to those seen on an organization chart and processes by which groups and individuals seek to set and control policy, implement decisions, and allocate resources to achieve institutional and state goals. The following discussion begins with selected overviews offering a broad picture of community college governance, followed by a nonexhaustive selection of references and resources describing related structures, processes, and outcomes.

Overviews of Community College Governance

The following sources offer an overview of American community college governance.

NEW DIRECTIONS FOR COMMUNITY COLLEGES, no. 141, Spring 2008 © 2008 Wiley Periodicals, Inc.
Published online in Wiley InterScience (www.interscience.wiley.com) • DOI: 10.1002/cc.318

Cohen, A. M., and Brawer, F. B. *The American Community College.* (4th ed.) San Francisco: Jossey-Bass, 2003.

This book offers an interpretive analysis of the identities and relationships of various entities in community college governance, including college administration, faculty collective bargaining units, governing boards, state coordinating boards, regional accrediting agencies, and federal funding sources. The authors observe that a lay board of trustees selects the college president who is responsible for implementing board policies in concert with administrators and faculty-staff committees. The board provides "the bridge between college and community, translating community needs for education into college policies and protecting the college from untoward external demands" (p. 124).

Davis, G. *Issues in Community College Governance.* Issues Paper no. 7. Washington, D.C.: American Association of Community Colleges, 2000.

Authored by the veteran director of the Illinois Community College Trustees Association, this paper examines current criticisms of community college governance and suggests some ways it could be improved. Because the challenges to governance are many, a solution to one problem could aggravate another and create new (and sometimes greater) difficulties for the college and those it serves. The author argues that it is better to acquire a full grasp of the problems before considering how they might all be solved. Advocates could strengthen community colleges by recognizing the increasing frequency of criticisms of governance and by advocating workable solutions.

Structures of Governance

All states have at least one statewide coordinating board for higher education established to coordinate statewide education planning, program approval and monitoring, and budget and policy recommendations to governors and legislatures. The following sources describe different ways of categorizing the organizational and funding structures of these governance systems.

Bowen, F. M., Bracco, K. R., Callan, P. M., Finney, J. E., Richardson, R. C., Jr., and Trombley, W. *State Structures for the Governance of Higher Education: A Comparative Study.* San Jose: California Higher Education Policy Center, 1998.

This report summarizes methodology, research design, and findings from a comparative study of postsecondary governance in seven states (California, Florida, Georgia, Illinois, Michigan, New York, and Texas). Defining a state system of higher education to include "elected officials, executive and legislative agencies, and state procedures for regulation and finance, as well as public and private postsecondary colleges and universities" (p. 4), the authors sought to understand how state governance structures affect performance and how governance structure affects the strategies that state policymakers devise as they encourage institutions to respond to contextual change and new state priorities.

Education Commission of the States. *State Profiles: Postsecondary Governance Structures.* Denver, Colo.: Education Commission of the States, 2007.
  The Postsecondary Governance Structures Database is a 2007 revision of the ECS 1997 *State Postsecondary Structures Sourcebook.* The database contains descriptions of state-level postsecondary education governance and coordination structures for all fifty states as well as links to related resources. The ECS web site (www.ecs.org) also offers selected references and readings on governance such as a work by McGuinness (2003) that describes three models of postsecondary coordination and governance structures in the states within which community colleges are situated.

Lovell, C. D., and Trouth, C. "State Governance Patterns for Community Colleges." In B. Townsend and D. Bragg (eds.), *ASHE Reader on Community Colleges.* (3rd ed.) Boston: Pearson Custom, 2006.
  The authors describe four state-level taxonomies of community college governance. In addition, they describe factors influencing statewide community college governance systems such as federal and state policies, board composition, articulation, and collective bargaining.

Tollefson, T. A. "Martorana's Legacy: Research on State Systems of Community Colleges." Paper presented at the 42nd Annual Meeting of the Council for the Study of Community Colleges, Washington, D.C., Apr. 2000.
  This paper describes community college state coordination and governance structures, mission evolution, state funding, and state control. Included near the end of this paper is a table of changes in state-level coordinating structures for public junior and community colleges between 1963 and 1999.

Typologies of Funding

Community college boards are responsible for the resources, performance, and welfare of the institutions they govern. Effective governance aligns resource allocation policies and practices with state and local agendas for higher education. The following references describe types or models of community college funding.

Kenton, C. P., Schuh, J. H., Huba, M. E., and Shelly, M. C. "Funding Models of Community Colleges in 10 Midwest States." *Community College Review,* 2004, 32(3), 1–17.
  The authors describe four models of funding in community colleges found in ten Midwest states between 1990 and 2000. Implications for practice are discussed.

Mullin, C. M., and Honeyman, D. S. "The Funding of Community Colleges: A Typology of State Funding Formulas." *Community College Review,* 2007, *35*(2), 113–127.

This study develops a typology of community college funding formulas placing forty-eight states in three categories and five subcategories.

Palmer, J. "Funding the Multipurpose Community College in an Era of Consolidation." In D. S. Honeyman, J. L. Wattenbarger, and K. C. Westbrook (eds.), *A Struggle to Survive: Funding Higher Education in the Next Century.* Thousand Oaks, Calif.: Corwin, 1996.

Community college funding directly influences campus operations. This paper examines some benefits and funding tradeoffs between typical college functions of access, education, and social service agency.

Richardson, R. C., Jr., and Leslie, L. L. *The Impossible Dream? Financing Community College's Evolving Mission.* Washington, D.C.: American Association of Community and Junior Colleges, 1980.

This three-part monograph discusses relationships between mission and funding. The first part describes components of the community college mission including transfer, vocational education, developmental or remedial education, continuing education, community service, and contract education. The second part discusses the history of community college funding, highlighting gaps relative to evolving student needs. The third part contains recommendations for resolving conflict between aspirations for continuing mission development and financial constraints.

Processes of Governance

Governance is a function of structure and of how people act within that structure. In fact, institutional culture, trust, involvement, and communication within and between constituencies may be as important as the structures of governance in fostering desired outcomes (Minor and Tierney, 2005). The following resources discuss this process in greater detail.

Bensimon, E. M., and Neumann, A. *Redesigning Collegiate Leadership: Teams and Teamwork in Higher Education.* Baltimore, Md.: Johns Hopkins, 1993.

Using a study of fifteen institutions of higher education (three of which are community colleges), the authors explore and describe a collaborative leadership "not in terms of single individuals but in terms of teams."

Fryer, T. W., and Lovas, J. C. *Leadership in Governance: Creating Conditions for Successful Decision Making in the Community College.* San Francisco: Jossey-Bass, 1991.

In this study of nine community colleges, the authors identify some characteristics and attributes common to effective community college governance processes such as clarity, openness, fairness, competence, and stability. Terms like *leadership*—the art of getting others to want to do something that the leaders are convinced ought to be done in service of an institution's mission—and *governance*—the institution's processes for decision making and the communication related to them—are defined and clarified.

Hamilton, N. W. "Faculty Involvement in System-wide Governance." In W. G. Tierney (ed.), *Competing Conceptions of Academic Governance.* Baltimore, Md.: Johns Hopkins, 2004.
This chapter discusses how faculty are involved in governance at the system level and uses case studies of shared governance operations in California, Georgia, Minnesota, and North Carolina to identify common themes and to discuss related governance structures.

Hull, J. R., and Keim, M. C. "Nature and Status of Community College Leadership Development Programs." *Community College Journal of Research and Practice,* 2007, *31*(9), 689–702.
In this study a survey was mailed to a national sample of 389 incumbent community college presidents to gather data about community college leadership development programs. From the study's response rate of 74 percent, the most cited national and regional development programs included the Chair Academy (designed by the department chairs of the Maricopa Community Colleges for aspiring or current department chairs), the Executive Leadership Initiative (developed by the League for Innovation in Community Colleges for aspiring presidents), and the Future Leaders Institute (sponsored by the American Association of Community Colleges for midlevel administrators). Nearly 70 percent of presidents reported a need to expand in-house development programs.

Kater, S., and Levin, J. S. "Shared Governance in Community Colleges in the Global Economy." Paper presented at the annual meeting of the American Educational Research Association, New Orleans, Apr. 2002.
Kater and Levin conducted a document analysis of 237 collective bargaining agreements (representing faculty at 301 community colleges in twenty-two states). They identified sixteen governance areas, including budget, calendar, curriculum, discipline, evaluation, and tenure. This study suggests that collective bargaining procedures have expanded rather than limited faculty's influence of and participation in governance.

Petty, G. F. (ed.). *Active Trusteeship for a Changing Era.* New Directions for Community Colleges, no. 51. San Francisco: Jossey-Bass, 1985.
The author discusses the role of trustees in addressing internal and external pressures on community colleges. It includes a discussion of trustees' roles in congressional lobbying, as advocates in state legislatures, and in accreditation proceedings.

Richardson, R. C., Jr., Blocker, C. E., and Bender, L. W. *Governance for the Two-Year College.* Englewood Cliffs, N.J.: Prentice-Hall, 1972.

In a world where everything old seems new again, this book from the 1970s offers a good deal of information helpful for understanding and working with present-day governance issues. While some of the specifics in this discussion have changed, much of the general theory and perspective on participative or shared governance at national, regional, state, and local levels remains pertinent.

Smart, J. C., Kuh, G. D., and Tierney, W. G. "The Roles of Institutional Cultures and Decision Approaches in Promoting Organizational Effectiveness in Two-Year Colleges." In B. Townsend and D. Bragg (eds.), *ASHE Reader on Community Colleges.* (3rd ed.) Boston: Pearson Custom, 2006.

This study, based on data from a stratified random sample of thirty public two-year colleges, explores the relative influence of factors in the external environment, institutional culture, and internal decision-making and managerial approaches on the organizational effectiveness of community colleges. The authors conclude that the indirect influences of these factors on effectiveness may have been underestimated in the past and that attention to institutional cultures and decision approaches may reduce negative influences of factors such as declining funding and enrollment.

Weisman, I. M., and Vaughan, G. B. (eds.). *Presidents and Trustees in Partnership: New Roles and Leadership Challenges.* New Directions for Community Colleges, no. 98. San Francisco: Jossey-Bass, 1997.

The authors describe national demographic profiles of governing boards and presidents of community colleges, their roles, and relationships. A model orientation and professional development program for trustees is proposed and recommendations made to improve leadership and governance.

Outcomes of Governance

Logically speaking, the core mission of an educational institution is the education of its students. Studies of campus governance typically ignore student outcomes, whereas the more voluminous research on student outcomes rarely looks at governance dynamics and processes. Recent studies have begun bridging this gap.

Berger, J. B. "Organizational Behavior at Colleges and Student Outcomes: A New Perspective on College Impact." *The Review of Higher Education,* 2000, 23(2), 177–198.

The author of this paper observes that "most existing applications of organization theory to the study of higher education concentrate on academic leadership, governance, and organizational effectiveness, . . . regard[ing] student experiences and outcomes only as secondary considerations" (p. 177). Berger outlines a framework in which academic governance and leadership are assessed primarily according to their ability to help colleges provide educationally sound environments for students.

Jackson, J. F., and Kile, K. S. "Does a Nexus Exist Between the Work of Administrators and Student Outcomes in Higher Education? An Answer from a Systematic Review of Research." *Innovative Higher Education,* 2004, 28(4), 285–301.

The simple answer to the question posed in the title of this informative review of the literature is "we don't know because we haven't looked." This review provides support for paying "closer attention to the interplay between student, personal, and institutional outcomes as it relates to the work of administrators."

Terenzini, P. T., and Reason, D. "Parsing the First Year of College: A Conceptual Framework for Studying College Impacts." Paper presented at the meeting of the Association for the Study of Higher Education, Philadelphia, Nov. 2005.

Focusing on the first year of college, when student attrition rates are highest, this paper proposes a conceptual framework to assess influences not usually considered in studies of student learning, such as faculty cultures, internal structures, and program and policy considerations. The proposed model suggests that the relevant internal organizational features fall generally into three categories: internal structures, policies, and practices; academic and student affairs program policies and practices; and the faculty culture.

Titus, M. A. "No College Student Left Behind: The Influence of Financial Aspects of a State's Higher Education Policy on College Completion." *The Review of Higher Education,* 2006, 29(3), 293–317.

The author asserts that if the institution is not succeeding in educating students, the board and the CEO must look at their own performance as leadership team. Positive assessments of board and CEO performance mean little if their colleges are in trouble.

Concluding Remarks

These are challenging times for community colleges. Embedded in a complex array of historic, social, economic, and political forces, the do-everything-for-everyone mission of comprehensive community colleges is meeting increased resistance from larger, more diverse student populations, unreliable funding structures, and escalating expectations of institutional accountability for student outcomes. Yet for many students "the choice is not between the community college and a senior residential institution; it is between the community college and nothing" (Cohen and Brawer, 2003, p. 53). Effective governance bridges individual and community needs for education with the college policies and practices necessary to achieve those ends.

References

Cohen, A. M., and Brawer, F. B. *The American Community College.* (4th ed.) San Francisco: Jossey-Bass, 2003.

McGuinness, A. C. *ECS State Notes: Models of Postsecondary Education Coordination and Governance in the States.* Denver, Colo.: Education Commission of the States, 2003.

Minor, J. T., and Tierney, W. G. "The Danger of Deference: A Case of Polite Governance." *Teachers College Record,* 2005, *107*(1), 137–156.

PAM SCHUETZ *is a postdoctoral fellow at the Institute for Policy Research at Northwestern University.*

NEW DIRECTIONS FOR COMMUNITY COLLEGES • DOI: 10.1002/cc

INDEX

rural resource differential in policy decisions are key for rural campuses. Furthermore, the similarities between large rural institutions and suburban institutions present a nexus for opportunities to share information on best practices and provide a basis for collaboration. This volume identifies issues rural leaders will likely encounter on their campuses and provides a set of tools and strategies to address those issues.
ISBN: 978-07879-97205

CC136   **Community College Missions in the 21st Century**
Barbara K. Townsend, Kevin J. Dougherty
Authors examine both long-standing and emerging societal and functional missions of community colleges. Are traditional missions still relevant? Should the focus be postsecondary education for students who might not otherwise obtain it, or the needs of the local community including business and industry? Providing transfer education? Workforce training and continuing education? This volume's chapters will stimulate thinking and discussion among policymakers, leaders, scholars, and educators.
ISBN: 0-7879-9575-4

CC135   **Pathways To and From the Community College**
Debra D. Bragg, Elisabeth A. Barnett
Examines local, state, and federal programs to help underserved students enter and succeed in college. Focuses on "academic pathways," boundary-spanning curricula, instructional strategies, and organizational structures to link high schools with two- and four-year colleges. The academic pathways support students during transitions and can be alternate routes to educational attainment. Topics include dual enrollment, dual credit, early and middle college high schools, plus career and technical education pathways and emerging models.
ISBN: 0-7879-9422-7

CC134   **Benchmarking: An Essential Tool for Assessment, Improvement, and Accountability**
Jeffrey A. Seybert
Comparing your institution's performance to that of its peers is a critical part of assessing institutional effectiveness and student learning outcomes. Two-year colleges now have access to national data collection and reporting consortia to identify and benchmark with peer schools. This volume describes the costs and benefits of benchmarking, the newly available community college data, and how your institution can use it for assessment and improvement.
ISBN: 0-7879-8758-1

CC133   **Latino Educational Opportunity**
Catherine L. Horn, Stella M. Flores, Gary Orfield
Latinos enroll at community colleges at rates higher than any other racial or ethnic group. Many factors influence Latino education—immigration policy, language, academic opportunity, family—and, despite research, the influence of these factors remains confounding. This issue explains the ways and extent to which community colleges can provide Latino students with access and opportunity.
ISBN: 0-7879-8624-0

New Directions for Community Colleges
Order Form
SUBSCRIPTIONS AND SINGLE ISSUES

DISCOUNTED BACK ISSUES:

Use this form to receive **20% off** all back issues of New Directions for Community Colleges. All single issues are priced at **$23.20** (normally $29.00).

TITLE   ISSUE NO.   ISBN

_____   _____   _____

_____   _____   _____

_____   _____   _____

Call 888-378-2537 or see mailing instructions below. When calling, mention the promotional code JB7ND to receive your discount.

SUBSCRIPTIONS: *(1 year, 4 issues)*

☐ New Order   ☐ Renewal

U.S.	☐ Individual: $80	☐ Institutional: $195
Canada/Mexico	☐ Individual: $80	☐ Institutional: $235
All Others	☐ Individual: $104	☐ Institutional: $269

Call 888-378-2537 or see mailing and pricing instructions below. Online subscriptions are available at www.interscience.wiley.com.

Copy or detach page and send to:
John Wiley & Sons, Journals Dept, 5th Floor
989 Market Street, San Francisco, CA 94103-1741

Order Form can also be faxed to: 888-481-2665

Issue/Subscription Amount: $ _____

Shipping Amount: $ _____
(for single issues only—subscription prices include shipping)

Total Amount: $ _____

SHIPPING CHARGES:		
SURFACE	Domestic	Canadian
First Item	$5.00	$6.00
Each Add'l Item	$3.00	$1.50

(No sales tax for U.S. subscriptions. Canadian residents, add GST for subscription orders. Individual rate subscriptions must be paid by personal check or credit card. Individual rate subscriptions may not be resold as library copies.)

☐ Payment enclosed (U.S. check or money order only. All payments must be in U.S. dollars.)

☐ VISA ☐ MC ☐ Amex # _____ Exp. Date _____

Card Holder Name _____ Card Issue # _____

Signature_____ Day Phone _____

☐ Bill Me (U.S. institutional orders only. Purchase order required.)

Purchase order # _____
           Federal Tax ID13559302   **GST 89102 8052**

Name_____

Address _____

Phone _____ E-mail _____

NEW DIRECTIONS FOR COMMUNITY COLLEGES IS NOW AVAILABLE ONLINE AT WILEY INTERSCIENCE

What is Wiley InterScience?

Wiley InterScience is the dynamic online content service from John Wiley & Sons delivering the full text of over 300 leading scientific, technical, medical, and professional journals, plus major reference works, the acclaimed *Current Protocols* laboratory manuals, and even the full text of select Wiley print books online.

What are some special features of Wiley InterScience?

Wiley InterScience Alerts is a service that delivers table of contents via e-mail for any journal available on Wiley InterScience as soon as a new issue is published online.

Early View is Wiley's exclusive service presenting individual articles online as soon as they are ready, even before the release of the compiled print issue. These articles are complete, peer-reviewed, and citable.

CrossRef is the innovative multi-publisher reference linking system enabling readers to move seamlessly from a reference in a journal article to the cited publication, typically located on a different server and published by a different publisher.

How can I access Wiley InterScience?

Visit http://www.interscience.wiley.com

Guest Users can browse Wiley InterScience for unrestricted access to journal Tables of Contents and Article Abstracts, or use the powerful search engine.

Registered Users are provided with a *Personal Home Page* to store and manage customized alerts, searches, and links to favorite journals and articles. Additionally, Registered Users can view free Online Sample Issues and preview selected material from major reference works.

Licensed Customers are entitled to access full-text journal articles in PDF, with select journals also offering full-text HTML.

How do I become an Authorized User?

Authorized Users are individuals authorized by a paying Customer to have access to the journals in Wiley InterScience. For example, a university that subscribes to Wiley journals is considered to be the Customer. Faculty, staff and students authorized by the university to have access to those journals in Wiley InterScience are Authorized Users. Users should contact their Library for information on which Wiley journals they have access to in Wiley InterScience.

ASK YOUR INSTITUTION ABOUT WILEY INTERSCIENCE TODAY!

CPSIA information can be obtained at www.ICGtesting.com
Printed in the USA
BVOW02s0722241213

339964BV00008B/86/P